AF225594

Days of Soup
and Holler

Liesl Garner

Days of Soup and Holler

First Edition: 2021

ISBN: 9781524315733
ISBN eBook: 9781524315832

© of the text:
   Liesl Garner

©of the images:
   Growing up in a Castle; I am Woman, Dance Me!; I Have Been Waiting
   my Whole Entire Life for this Moment!: Shutterstock.com
   Pot. Kettle. Black.; Mothers; All this Talk of Rosemary and Religion:
   morguefile.com
   Strengthen me with Raisins: Scott Garner
   Benediction; I Was a Dark Storm Cloud; Boomerangs for Sale;
   Christmas in Deep Freeze; Say Yes; Great and Simple Images that Open
   our Hearts; Constantly Knocking Over the Teacups: Liesl Garner

© Layout, design and production of this edition: 2021 EBL Books

Table of Contents

Section Three:
Wild, Crazy Children

Section Four:
A Poet Peeks Out at the World

Section Five:
Finding Home in a Community of Writers

SECTION ONE:

EARLY YEARS

She Saw Elephants

She saw Pink Elephants
running through the house
eating Pickle Jars.
She'd talk to herself graciously
in the mirror at the end of the hall,
"You go first," "No, after you."

She once thought I was a young man
with a crush on her, after I'd been
visiting her all day with a new haircut.
She told my mother I was the janitor,
that I lived in the basement,
and that I was "sweet on her."

She'd get agitated and say
she had to go see Mama.
She had to catch a train.
Though Mama had been dead
for thirty years;
I'd calm her and say
the trains weren't running tonight
because of the fog,
but we'd get her on the first one
in the morning.

By morning, she'd have forgotten.

I helped her build an elaborate,
unreal world,
because the real world for her
was nurses, and medicine,
and bed sores, and night terrors,
and memories of long-ago,
people who were
now dead.

She taught me, without knowing,
to make-believe
when the real world was ugly or lonely;
to say something is when it's not,
if that makes things more interesting,
or not when it is,
if that makes life more bearable.

And I'm not crazy yet — but I'll know
how to manage when I get there.

I sang her to sleep,
rubbed the worry out of her forehead,
stroked her hands until her fists
would relax, her gnarled fingers
would spread out on the sheets
and her breathing would loosen
the grip around her heart.

I don't think she ever once
knew who I was.

Every time I visited, she thought
I was someone different.
In Junior High, I didn't know
who I was either,
so, we agreed, and I was happy.

I wish I could have been there
when she died.
Living a dream world for her,
to keep her calm,
was mostly what kept me sane
through my teens.

And now, her sister, my grandmother,
is seeing Elephants,
and talking to invisible couples
who have stopped by for a visit.

If I ever marry, I'll try to remember
to tell my intended
that make-believe runs in my family.

Growing up in a Castle

I grew up *playing* in a castle. My parents were members of an organization whose headquarters was an actual castle, and as little children, my sisters and I played all over that place and ran up winding staircases, then down again into the kitchens far below. There were secret passageways and huge chandeliers. There were tall, elegant windows with heavy draperies we could hide behind. It was our playground.

There is something so perfect and lovely about the memories I have of playing there. We may have only really been at the headquarters on five or six occasions, but the way I remember it, it was an enormous part of my childhood. Perhaps because I played there often whether we were there in person or not. I was a princess with long flowing hair and gowns and little velvet slippers. That is what I dreamed of myself.

When we visited the ocean on the West Coast for the first time, I was 13 and oh, so dramatic. I brought along a billowing skirt and a scarf because I wanted to be photographed looking out at the waves, with the wind in my hair, and my skirt and scarf fluttering in the breeze. I have always had a vivid imagination, and a poet's heart.

A writing exercise from Natalie Goldberg in Writing Down the Bones, asks, "Where do you come from, who are you, what makes you you?" For me, that includes *growing up in a castle*, because that is what I feel is true, not just that I *played* there on a handful of occasions, but that I grew up there... *That* is owning whatever I want and then letting it go, as Natalie says to do. And I believe it shaped me to some degree. It has something to do with my love of the dramatic, my pension for romanticizing memories, my living in a dreamworld. Some of my favorite writers have said that they dislike living in reality. Fiction can be so much more fun.

"Own anything you want and then let it go."

The problem is that my family has gotten into play arguments with me about this phrasing. They've said, "You said you grew up in a castle." And I've countered, "No, I said I grew up *Playing* in a castle." After all this time, I think I may have to concede, that I very clearly told them something from my delusional remembrance of my growing up. I may actually have claimed to have grown up in a castle.

Before the Rebellion

It was the summer of apple pies.
Summer of swinging from my knees
upside down in the apple tree
in the backyard, the last summer of being
a carefree kid. I don't remember it ever
being too hot, because I baked every day,
perfecting my crust until it flaked
just looking at it.

People were amazed by my apple pies.
We served them to friends and family
gathered around our table in the
cool of the evening — talking late into
the night because that's how our
table always was, bright and cozy,
and loud talking.

It was the first time I'd ever felt shy,
always before I'd join in easily
with the grown-up talk, precocious,
curious child that I was, but just
on the verge of teenager, I was lanky
and strung out — long armed and legged,
long neck all spindly — no longer

at ease with my body, I would perch
on the sidelines and listen and long
to be a part. Deep Philosophical
conversations between plates
of my perfect apple pie, and there
were always comments, asides,
"how delicious," my only entry
into the conversation, my input.
In my head, I was being excluded.
It was the beginning of teenaged drama,
feeling alone and unwanted. I was right
there in the middle of our glorious table
of conversation — everyone with a fork,
scraping the last crumbs off their plates,
but I couldn't open my mouth to speak.

It was the last summer for a long time
that I would be a part — that I added to
rather than take away. Every afternoon,
all summer long, I spent hours picking,
peeling, chopping, rolling out the dough,
pinching the edges of the crust all around
the pie pan for a perfect scalloped edge,
making little cutouts of art in the top,
and packing all those juicy apples
in between — with pats of butter.

Prodigal Daughter

(Written in my twenties — so much has changed since then —
but it is one of my parents' favorites)

But the Bible doesn't tell us
if the good brother
and the Prodigal Son
ever bridged the chasm of hurt
to be close again.
As a Prodigal Daughter,
this bothers me.

For the sisters that never strayed
but ached for me
and the hurt I caused everyone,
anger burns near the surface
every time I come home.

The son came home once
after years of hard living
and that's the end of the story.
This daughter has built
a revolving door — has never
stayed home long
after the celebration.

But, still hurting, leaves again.
Can't bear the hurt
of the sister's that stayed.
Keeps thinking maybe next time,
the reunion will be sweet and genuine.

I keep hoping for a penance
that will be real — Strong enough
and harsh enough to prove
how I long for the fellowship
of family.
But each horrid downfall
widens the gap.

Oh, to be young again!
To build forts and climb trees
with my sisters,
to laugh and wrestle with dad,
and cozy down to listen
to the melodic voice
of mom reading.

What made me want to leave
this happy home, I'll never know,
but the road back keeps getting longer,
the sisters get further shrouded
in the mist.

I don't know the magic words
to bring them closer.

Too many years and too many hurts.

I've lost track of all there is
to apologize for.
"Sorry" has lost its meaning,
but I am lost without them,
the three who stayed.

A double-edged sword,
a catch-22 — I can't stay
unless I know they want me...
They can't trust to want me
unless they know I mean to stay.

I see now there can be
no compromise!
It was I who broke the
bridge of trust, and it will be I
who must restore it.

Why must it be a bridge
which may take years to build?

If I had only damaged
a step on the front porch,
think how quickly I could mend it —
and run inside for dinner —
I would hardly be missed!

They have been missing me
for years, thought.

The bridge is ornate — a thing
of beauty once repaired.

I am overwhelmed at the task
before me — the skills I must learn.

But I am told there is
a Master Craftsman
who will teach me...

Picnic Tree

Across a field from the dorms, a hike,
up a hill, and lost, or nearly,
we trudged until we found again
the Picnic Tree.
Vast, enormous, with perches
and arms outstretched to hold us,
tuck us in, and secure us
as we lounged, draped all around
and up and down that tree.
Five girls at a time, or more, each
with a snack, and a daydream,
a crush to speak of in code.
There was never a wind; a hush
surrounded us. The forest listened
and held our secrets dear;
looked into our hearts, our longings,
whispered promises over us
of someday, our own.

But What of the Other Mothers?

(For Andrea — Mother's Day 1994 — when we were both
waiting tables and her son was in Hawaii)

Sunday — blazing sun
Tall, cool teas at brunch
Flowers on the tables
Moms with their clans
Cards and presents litter the aisles
Waiters dodge baby strollers

But what of the Other Mothers?
The ones whose love pierces them today
Sharp pains tug at arms and hearts
Arms ache to hold the little one
Hearts break to see a face, hear a word
Baby is with Daddy today
or Grandma or a family who was
ready for a child when she was not

Mothers — almost more so for the yearning
for the chores they're unable to perform
for the tears they miss wiping

for the lullabies someone else gets to sing

Happy Mother's Day Sweetheart!
Shed a tear or sing a song
But know that you are loved —
The title of Mother — earned by
battle scars on the heart — is yours!

Say a prayer for Other Mothers
whose love makes them lonely
who serve brunch to big families
and smile — but sadly — because
Baby is with Daddy.

My Life Story in Music

This was originally published in the Valley Voices section of the Fresno Bee on October 20, 2001. It was written several years before that. It seems like a lifetime ago that these dark sounds could have resonated with me so powerfully. Today, I am such an upbeat, cheerful person. However, it is a much-requested piece of writing among friends and family, so I am sharing it again.

Several years ago, a friend and I went to see a concert with a classical piece by Beethoven and a more modern piece by 20th century composer, Alfred Schnittke, performed at Davies Symphony Hall in San Francisco. I was pretty sure I would hate the modern piece, because I do not like cacophony for the sake of being loud and noisy and "artsy" — but I was completely blown away. It was my life story in music.

There was a female Viola soloist, a full symphony, a harpsichord, up-right piano, grand piano and a harp. (Let me fast forward and say that afterward, I met several people who had hated it, but once I shared what I had been seeing — the story I followed throughout the piece, they loved it!) This is what I "saw."

The violist was the main character of the story. This was her life, and the orchestra was "The World" or "Bad Experiences in Life." She would play beautifully and then little by little, some instrument in the orchestra would start chiming in at the wrong time, in the wrong chord, completely dissonant. She would shrug it off and keep playing, but the orchestra (the world) would get louder and louder and burst into some horrific sounding stuff. It would almost drown her out.

If you continued watching only her, you would see the orchestra finally start to influence her. Even her body movements would show the effect. Her shoulders would hunch forward, her face would contort, and slowly, her music would become ugly. The orchestra would die out completely and all that would be left was her dreadful sound, dragging and crying and tortured. She was all alone and punishing herself for the ugliness of the world.

Then she would begin to get a grip on things. Her music would become lovely again. Sometimes the three pianos would play along with her and she would be in sync with the world. The orchestra would even become beautiful. But then it would run amok and gain speed and get completely out of control again.

This happened over and over again, and each time it seemed harder for the soloist to regain a beauty after the outburst of the world. At one point, the orchestra went completely hysterical, grinding and screaming and sounding horrendous. She was trying so hard to be heard over the chaos. She was even standing taller and stretching upward. The music wouldn't let up and finally... she stopped. She bowed her head.

I had tears in my eyes. I was on the edge of my seat. I was begging her not to let the world win, not to let it silence her or stop her music. After a moment of agony (on my part), she raised her head, thrust her shoulders back and began plucking the strings. I wanted to cheer! "Bravo! She's still got her sense of humor!"

Back and forth and over and over again, the world thrust terrible things at her. Sometimes she would prevail and remain beautiful throughout the interruptions, and sometimes she would give in and be destroyed.

But she was never actually silenced. In the end, she held one note for almost two minutes, gradually softening, gracefully ending her song.

I was beside myself. I wanted to jump out of my seat and cheer and scream. But most of the audience hadn't understood it and I was sad that the applause was not as enthusiastic as I would have liked. The orchestra stood and applauded her though. They had understood the story, or at least her talent.

I was moved by this strange music more than any piece I have ever heard. My friend, Brian, kept nodding off and afterwards I told him that "This was my life story!"

"Oh," he yawned, "that's why I kept falling asleep then. I've heard it before."

It was magnificent and I feel I learned a lot. I got to see someone else living my chaotic life. I got to see her triumph and fall apart. I wept and cheered for her. She was so beautiful and so strong, so weak and hurting, all swept together and intertwined.

Leaving

And I'll kiss my
deck goodbye
Here where the words
finally came

Where pen touched paper
and tears could be read
Where I learned to
pray again

My refuge in the
storm of feelings
Where I awakened
and stretched toward morning

My deck has embraced me
at all hours
of the day and night
when the muse was heavy

It's shared in all the process
The anger, the hurt,
the remembering
The joy and reborn wonder

How do I say
good-bye to a place?
To the feelings I've had
in this place?

It's only a place
It has no feelings or memories
But it has been my closest friend
I'll kiss my deck good-bye!

Lila Fae Hancock

(From my long-ago single days)

Johnny with the bodacious burgundy hair
is making pizzas
at Golden Boys in North Beach.
Talk of poetry and politics fills the air,
literature captures our imaginations.
We drink Red Tail Ale and debate and flirt.

In walks a street woman
to wash in the bathroom.
An odor surrounds her as she moves past.
I catch a glimpse of what seem like
rows and rows of yellow teeth.
We feel superior
because it hurts to empathize.
We're all young and strong
and have jobs and dreams still.

Chatter stops when she comes back
through the room.
She's invading the comfort
of our intellectually elite mood.
She comes toward me, asking for a cigarette.

She leans against my stool,
so close I can feel her breath.
I hurriedly reach for a smoke,
I just want her to leave.

She stops — she's standing so close.
She starts to sway — she starts to croon.
I'm frightened.
Aretha Franklin sings about
a Pink Cadillac on the jukebox.
The woman at my side is harmonizing.

In a powerful, robust, aching voice she sings
and I am mesmerized.

I tentatively sing the melody
and she reaches for my hand.
Her tiny, knobbled hand holds
my polished and manicured fingers
and there's no one else around...
We're making music and she calls me,
"Sister."

She's no longer scary and ugly and scarred.
She's a woman I want to know more about.
I listen as she tells me stories.

Her name is Lila Fae Hancock, and I tell her
she's Sassy, Saucy, Smart...
and Soulful, she adds.

We sing some more, arms around each other.

When the chairs are being stacked
on the tables,
I walk her to the door — she reaches up
with one hand on each side of my face
and kisses my cheek.

She says, "You're the first person
that's shown me any love."
My eyes sting and I feel
more awake than I have in years.

I've never seen her again, though I've looked.
I sink into quiet memories
when self-righteous talk
moves to the homeless.

Somewhere out there is a woman
with a beautiful voice
who called me "Sister" and kissed me,
and for a moment I loved her.
I wonder if she remembers.

SECTION TWO:

THEN CAME
LOVE —MARRIED LIFE

I am Woman, Dance Me!

As I chop and dice to a beat;
close the door with a foot,
a drawer with a hip,
and turn to rinse a radish.

Dinner prep is never as fun
as when you're watching
and adoring me
and burping the baby
while I cook.

There is nothing sexier
than a man who can help
with the kids, or pick up a frying pan
and sauté and sizzle and shake it up
over a hot stove.

You make music with every grind
of the peppermill and you know
I'm watching,
so you grind a little more
and look over your shoulder
and yeah, I see you,
and I'm bouncing
a baby on my hip,
or getting caught in spider webs
and having a three-year old
superhero rescue me.

In a house full of kids
there is always a beat going on somewhere.
There's "Spiderman, Spiderman, does
whatever a spider can," — being sung
for the 82nd time in a row,
or spoons being banged on a table,
stomps of delight,
or squeals of laughter,
and we learn to embrace it
and dance along. Over the hubbub,
from across the room,
we catch eyes. Our sons
like to Air High Five and we've learned
to Air Tango with dips and swirls,
a rose in your mouth
and that look in your eye.

You still spin me over the noise and
the racket, over dinner, dishes, diapers,
or irritated kids recovering in a calm-out.

Narnia Today

Wardrobes make me swoon with longing.
There is a hush and a pause before I creak open the door
to look inside, my heart flutters in anticipation
of maybe, just maybe, a peek into Narnia — a getting lost
in another world and growing up there, and finding
my bravery fighting battles beside dwarfs and dryads,
dancing on snowy lawns or
dew-drenched glens under a moonlit sky,
with wood-nymphs and satyrs playing flutes.

All my life I've been one chance encounter away from being
swept up into magic — by staring
at a gorgeous ship at sea painting,
or following a path into a wood, or opening a wardrobe door
and peeking inside, past the coats and the moth balls,
stretching my hand back to where it becomes
no longer coats or the back of a bureau as expected,
but bristles of pine trees and the snap of cold and snow in the air.
And while I've never been gone for years and come back
before anyone noticed I was gone — I have been gone
for long afternoons.

My husband was up in a tree once, spooked and overthinking,
because the angle of the limb he was cutting,
and the physics of the fall,
and the proximity of the roof and patio and electric line
were all conspiring to kill him. From his vantage point, he saw
a yard sale several houses away and a wardrobe
befitting adventurous imaginings for me. He climbed down,
marched over, arranged a trade for some tree trimming there,
and climbed back up his scary tree and called me from the top
to explain his negotiations and how love for me, and desire
to bring home this prize for me — this every child's longing
for an access point and a wardrobe of my own — was giving him
the impetus to handle business on the tree that had him unnerved.

Narnia inspired the trimming of that dangerous tree
and Narnia brought my husband home,
bureau in arms for me. I think every home with children
or grandchildren should have a wardrobe
that is off limits, of course,
because that only makes the sneaking toward it,
the built-up anticipation,
afternoons of daydreaming, planning and adventuring —
the fear and hope and longing stronger.

Sit Yourself DOWN Girl

Sit yourself Down Girl
for a little while
for a poem that begs your caress.
A little rest, a little rebirth
astride that Pony Gallup
Engine Rev...
The wind on your face,
the road laid out before you
like a ribbon of darkness;
dancing out there
in the off and beyond,
a tickle, a tease,
the enticement
around that next bend;
a series of curves
too good to be true.
Knee-hugging, seat-shifting
turns that race your heart
to a Righteous Place
of Awe and Beauty
of Beating Applause
to match the Eyes of Twinkle
that Defy
Issues of the Outside World.

Soundtrack: We all wish we had one!

(Written when I was mad at my husband and somehow talking in a Southern Accent made me forget)

I need a Harmonica
background,
a banjo or a steel guitar,
maybe a washboard making
a heap of noise behind
me as I croon about
my sorry tales,
or sweet hopes,
my pitiful poor excuses,
and my big ideas.

Syncopation would help,
don't you think?
Would make me sway
just a little, and be sassy
just a little, maybe talk
in a Southern drawl
and forget for a moment
that I was really hurtin' — 'cause

with a backdrop of sound
like that, it all becomes music,
and sorrow can beat out
a pulse to a blues song
like nobody's business.

Before long, I'm just
dancin' again, eyes closed,
head bent back, shoulders
rollin' — feet a tappin' — a big ol'
sloppy smile across
my sad face. And in the heat
of the moment, I might even
forget I'm mad, might wanna
rub up against you, breathe
deep the smell of you, say
somethin' saucy and ridiculous:
a murmur, a mumble, a sweet
little nothin' that turns into
somthin' and all of a sudden
I'm in love with you again!

Because of a Harmonica
and a poet's sense of justice,
that turns everything to good
again with a little bit o' rhythm.

Bared Claws

I have heard of the dance of Eagles mating.
I have seen the statue of talons out sharp;
a fierce battle and free fall — wings and bodies
tumbling over one another as they drop to earth.
Claws outstretched to tear and wrestle
and seconds before they crash with a fury and a splat,
they peel apart and soar upward again — circling
each other gracefully as they rise — intertwining
like ribbons, their movements fluid,
completely opposite from the downward fray.

When they reach the heights, they begin again.
Somehow, there is a tease, a ferocious front
and then a soft gliding against one another
In the upward motion. Perhaps they test each other
for fight worthiness — to see how the other will hold up
in a battle before they decide to rear young together.

You and I have bared our claws,
haven't we, my dear?
We have frightened on another
with our fierceness and have
come back together timidly
each offering a little tenderness

toward the other — maybe not
apologizing, but moving
more gently close again.

Right before we come all the way
to a landing that would break us,
we tear ourselves apart
and begin to rise.
We offer a smile and a soft word
and once again we are dancing.

We have proved we are fight worthy.
I believe an outside opponent
wouldn't stand a chance, and I trust
you wholeheartedly to guard
my nest and our young;
to someday teach them how to fly,
how to laugh, how to fight and how to love.

And there was Morning

The creating of a family
doesn't happen overnight.
New to marriage — late in life,
suddenly parenting teenagers
when I had clearly forgotten
my own wayward youth.
I'd somehow revised history
and I *always* kept my room clean,
helped around the house
and did my homework.

And there was evening,
and there was morning,
the first day.

My early arguments with the kids
ended with me collapsing
into tears and realizing I hadn't
started becoming responsible
or growing up until my mid-thirties.
They are already so far ahead of me.
We would make up with
bowls of ice cream on the
front porch — our porch swing

creaking quietly — stars twinkling
in the summer sky.

And there was evening,
and there was morning,
the second day.

For so long, I'd wanted a baby
of my own — so much pain
surrounded my twice
inhabited womb.
My third time leaving the hospital
after childbirth — I finally got
to leave with a baby in my arms.
That moment so rich and poignant,
so full for me of delight and joy,
terror of not knowing enough,
and yet knowing we would do anything
for this child. My husband getting it,
knowing just how deeply a poet mom
would feel this pathos.

And there was evening,
and there was morning,
the third day.

Ups and downs, joy and pain, all
that life has to offer, and we are
getting old for a little kid. We
creak and grown and
run low on energy.
We work all the time and are tired

constantly. We work and wait for our
business to become profitable.
We forget to have fun. We wrestle
with tension as a living thing.
Our candle wicks are frazzled
at both ends.

And then I miss a cycle. Dear God,
we're pregnant again, our fourth boy.

And there was evening,
and there was morning,
the fourth day.

Despite misgivings from the medical
community, because of my age,
and being a little worried
this would be more
than we could handle — He is a
waddling wiggle of pure joy — eats
us out of house and home
and laughs with his whole, entire body.
We change course.
We swim the tide.
We embrace the inevitable chaos
of a house full of kids — we put off
redecorating and celebrate
sticky fingers for a while.

And there was evening,
and there was morning,
the fifth day.

There is rebirth in marriage,
changes come slowly. We begin
as opposites attracting
and start to meld or mingle,
our thoughts take on
similarities.
We come to the same side of the
road — or an island in the middle
on issues. We sidle up next
to each other and breathe deep.
You spin me forward
and pull me back in,
and we love the
rhythm of our dance.

And there was evening,
and there was morning,
the sixth day.

And it's always about beginning,
isn't it? First, we set the stage,
lay our foundation,
and then sit back
to barbeque and watch
the children grow,
laugh at those chubby legs
and first steps. We imagine
celestial beings sit back
over their barbeque
and watch our first steps
as a family — watch
us grow and trackour

progress with numbers
up the door post. Cheer
our successes and bite their
nails when we are perched
on the edge of disaster —
stand ready to break our falls.

And there was evening,
and there was morning,
the seventh day.

We start to see the patterns
and know that although there
are dark patches, there are
sometimes nights with no moon,
eventually there is morning.

We proclaim it Very Good,
and on we go!

"Again you will take up your tambourines"

A promise from scripture
spoken in the midst
of tragedy, and terror
on every side; darkness
and gloom.

It has been a lonely battle
waged through
clenched-teeth love,
not willing to cave
because it's not always, "better."
There have been
days of, "or worse."

And yet, we promised,
and so, we built.
We forged ahead
and remembered how to smile.
We grew battle-weary
and learned to make up.
We laughed until we cried.

We smoothed our rough
edges, and stumbled
over rough terrain.
We are in this together
so, we learned to lean
and hold each other close.

> "Again you will take up your tambourines,
> and go out to dance with the joyful."

*Jeremiah 31:3—4

Strengthen me with Raisins

Refresh me with apples,
for I am faint with love.

Strengthen me for the long haul
because today I feel it
and I know there have been
days when I didn't.

There will be days again.
There will be moments
of exasperation,
exhaustion,

confusion,
and blame,
amid the moments
of wonder, amazement,
witty banter,
repartee
between equals.

By some great miracle
we survived a time
when we both wanted out.
We simply couldn't walk away
from what we'd built
together — what we
are combined — the sum
greater
that two parts alone.

We waded through 18 months
of not getting it,
of being on different waves
and different courses — of crossing
paths eleventy-seven times
a day and just not ever
finding a way to connect,
both lost and misunderstood.

Valentine's Day came and
you cooked for me, you helped
me put the kids to bed,
you participated.
I felt a tiny glimmer

of hope flick on
in the back of my heart,
I quick blew it out,
and shoved it behind a door,
didn't want to hurt even more,
thinking things were back to good.

Then you started telling
me our story — the story of
how we met, and what you
thought,
and how terrified you were,
and how speechless,
and how you pursued me anyway,
and how you finally found me
again.
And how we became friends,
and how you think
I'm beautiful
and then you were sitting
with me, with your arms
around me as I cried,
telling me you knew,
You Knew
how close we were
to capsizing,
how out and off we were,
how tired and lonely
I'd become
and all you ever wanted
was to see me smile
and know you were somehow

behind it,
behind that joy or that glow.

That loving me every day
for the rest of our lives
was all you wanted from life.

You swooped me sideways
all over again,
clumsy me,
I've tripped and fallen
for every word you said
and you just keep picking me up
and brushing away tears
and holding on tight
to our dreams.

Strengthen me so I can stay
hopeful and sure,
smiling back through
ups and downs,
let me always be
a little faint with love.

"Strengthen me with raisins, refresh me with apples, for I am
faint with love," is from Song of Solomon 2:5

Every Other Breath I Take

Every other sock is mismatched
Every other season is too hot

Every night I am awakened by one
or the other of my little guys

Every other meal is prepared by my husband,
who is the one in our home who can cook.
The kids eat well half the time.
The rest of the time, it's experiments
or flops by mom — made with love and creativity
but very little culinary skill.

Every other moment we are working —
either running our business or trying to stay
one step ahead of major repairs.

Every night we share dinner around the table,
daddy's humor, the kids laughing, friends welcome.

"Every other breath I take is my wife's," you said
to a client, then called to tell me
because you knew it sounded cheesy
but you meant it,

and I knew as soon as you told me
how truthful you were being.
Over the phone, I could hear
the tears in your eyes — that matched mine.

Every other breath I take is yours.

Benediction

All this magnificent sky
bordered by
mountains that capture
sunsets and accentuate
the beauty of a simple
sun going down —
outlined as they are
like an artist's paper cut-outs.

This is my writing table,
my place of worship, my proving
grounds for motherhood.
In all this wide sky,
in all this long view,

we roam and explore,
find treasures,
and run races down a forever
long driveway,
skin our knees,
fall off bikes,
argue over who won,
chase each other
with bad intentions,
get caught,
held back by
mom or dad keeping
us from another's more
furious moments,
tramp across fields
in our tall boots,
drop handfuls of half-smushed
blackberries into buckets,
and appear at the kitchen
with purple faces
ready to make pie.

These mountains — these
early morning red skies.
My cathedral,
my invocation or
call to worship.

The sprinkling of chicken feed,
each morning, my broken alabaster,
watering ducks and watching
them all waddle

through their rituals
of cleaning each feather
to fluff out
and settle down.

Little grubby hands reaching
up to grab mine on a
walk — to walk too close to me,
and hug a leg in mid-step
to trip us both. This is
mothering at its best;
when my kids can't get enough
of me. This is my vespers.
My sweetie standing behind me,
arms wrapped around me, pointing
out another day done well,
another vibrant painted sky.

"I Will Not Pretend That
My Hands Don't Work"

When Scott and I were first married, and setting up our home together, I was unpacking boxes of files to put into the office, and came across an envelope full of sentences he'd had his boys write as a consequence for behavior that got them into trouble. I sat on the floor flipping through these pages, laughing until I cried. Scott didn't ever just have them write, "I will not hit my brother." He always made the sentences loop around to make a second line, so that it was impossible to go down line by line saying, "I, I, I, I, — will, will, will, will," etc.

I found, "I will not get mad at my clothes," and could imagine a meltdown of dramatic proportions that came before the sentence writing.

My favorite was always, "I will not pretend that my hands don't work." Scott came home and found me looking through the pages, and started telling me stories of Joey, standing at the kitchen sink, literally trying to get out of doing the dishes by flopping his hands around and saying they didn't work.

A couple of weeks ago, Scott got ill, and I took on the daily milking of the goats for him so he could rest. By about day four, after milking two goats morning and night, my left hand was so non-cooperative, that I could go through all the proper motions to milk, and nothing was happening. My hand was weak from not doing this on a consistent basis, and it was all I could do that night to finish the job. I came in and told Scott about it, and he just smiled at me and said, "I will not pretend that my hands don't work."

So, after a week of handling the job, my hands have gained the strength to keep going, and I offered to do the milking in the morning as we are getting closer to colder weather, and it's dark in the morning. It makes no sense for Scott to go out there in the dark to do all the animal chores, and then go work all day in the cold, when I could let him sit in the house for a few more minutes in the morning, and handle all the animals after I've gotten everyone off to work and school.

Somehow, every morning when I'm milking the goats, this has become a mantra running repeatedly in my mind, "I will not pretend that my hands don't work."

And I started thinking of the other things I put off because I'm just being lazy or I don't want to manage being disciplined enough to do them. Like writing every day, because, as I've said over and over again throughout my life, writing is soul work for me. It keeps me grounded and it is my spiritual practice. It is the thing that helps me wrap words around thoughts floating in and out of reach and pull them close to gaze upon them and make sense of them.

Writing helps me view the world more poetically, more beautifully, more attentively. Writing as a daily exercise keeps my mind strong, and my heart in balance; it keeps dark thoughts from building up and becoming monsters. My children find me a better mom when I'm taking the time to do this for myself, and I can see them as the poems I am writing every day.

I often don't write, because I get busy, and then I don't know how to catch up, and I'm not going to bother with catching up. Life has been busy. The boys are bigger and louder and much more active, more inquisitive, and their play is rougher and crazier. It's a bit of a three-ring circus sometimes, which is all the more reason for me to sit down and find a center every day and lose myself in the page for a moment.

"I will not pretend that my hands don't work."

Toward Paper, Toward Pen

Recently, I learned...
After almost twelve years
of marriage, and countless poems
about the ups and downs, the trials
and joys of us, the him and me, and
his and mine and ours — the
combined parts that work so well.
The poems I've written about
motherhood, about finding time
in the middle of it all to relish
the smiles of my children.

Sitting here on our bed, with papers
strewn all around me — cataloguing
every emotion of our whole
life together. In the last month,
I learned, you shared,
at our little kitchen table,
to our oldest son, in the midst
of his own breakup, you shared
that in the beginning, you were
jealous — jealous of my poetry.
Somehow you thought I'd been
passionately alive and writing about

all that came before, and had run out
of words once we got married.

I just needed time to adjust. So much
of my writing before had been about
heartbreak and loss and being
forlorn. It took a while to get to the
point where I could write happy. And
then I was deeply entrenched, I
started seeing the highs and lows of
love, not just the mountaintops.
There were valleys we trudged
through and those helped me
find my voice again. The sadness was
familiar. Our babies brought me out
of darkness,
and then you. And then you.

Somewhere along the way,
you embraced all my poet heart
had to offer; my rough edges,
my diamonds, my tears,
and my wild banshee hollers
in the night. The whole vocabulary
you learned to see
as me — my way of seeing the world.
My breathing out and breathing in.

And you taught our boys
to know the signs,
and to prod their poet mama
with kindness, little shoves

toward paper, toward pen,
when my heart was in tatters,
or my sighs became audible,
when joy was splitting
me apart — I now have a family of
supporters,
who tell me I need to go write.

My in-laws search for ancestors
and tidbits of knowledge
from the past. My husband said
in hushed tones how lucky
future generations
would be to find this tapestry
of our lives, spelled out in journals,
and notebooks, or sheaves of paper
tucked between pages of cookbooks.

We have come full circle,
you and I, when you realized
this was not a part of me
I kept from you, but a part of me
that was necessary
to experience you,
to breathe you in, and hold you close,
to live each moment with you twice,
and then some.

The High Holy Now

I just — I woke up hungry
before light — before sunup
before kids everywhere,
in the still of darkness
in the close and move together
in the pull and tighten
in the warmth of our bed
and the cool of pushed back
sheets — let me get my
hands on you, in the rock
and breathe, in the hum
and sigh, in the time
that stretches to gather
all that came before us,
every grain of sand,
every quark and nuance
of galactic dust, every
distant star gazing
down — to now,
as time stands still,
holding only you and me
in this hourglass hollow
where you revere my
poet heart with wordless

whispered enchantments.

We have this peace,
this place between us,
through us, surrounding,
enveloping and sustaining us.
We could stay here forever.
Right here, right now.
All that ever was and
all that ever will be
enshrined
in this moment
until we start to
breathe again,
awake again, move
and moan again,
and it's dangerous
how good this is,
could be disastrous
the truth of this,
the blinding light
and otherworldly wow of it
that render me
numb and dumb and breathless
reaching out to
steady myself with you
and touch and feel your heartbeat
quaking —
the rumble and roar of us.

SECTION THREE:

WILD, CRAZY CHILDREN

"Warm Chocolate Milk,
not hot, Warm!"

Every morning for the last year, Benjamin has asked for "Warm Chocolate Milk, not hot, Warm." He is very specific about what he wants. And every time I hand him a sippy cup with milk that has been warmed to the specific temperature requested, he thanks me, takes a sip and says, "Mmmm, Perfect!" It is so sweet. I love these little rituals that he has created all by himself.

Lately, if I'm working with the baby, the task of making a "Warm Chocolate Milk, not hot, Warm," for Ben falls on my husband. He'll ask in all seriousness if Ben would like that with ice cubes, or with a slice of pizza in it, or with green beans, or shredded cheese. Whatever pops into his head, and Ben will flip out just a little bit, thinking that Daddy is going to destroy his perfect drink.

Then Scott brings in the drink — made to perfection, just like Ben likes it — and Ben will ask again what he put in it this time. This has become a new tradition no matter who is serving his drink — we all play along. This morning it was my turn, I answered, "Broccoli and Bean Sprouts." He took the first sip, replied, "Mmmm, Perfect. Maybe that was the right thing to do." This is now what he says every time.

He is such a creature of habit — and apparently, so are the rest of us. We like knowing what to expect, and what is expected of us.

We just wish we could get the baby on board with all this keeping of habits. I thought we were there. For the last two nights, I've put him in his crib, and he's just grabbed his Wuuby and snuggled in and gone to sleep. Voila! So easy. It's been months of working up to this and having to rock him and walk him and let him cry a little, until he realized that sleep is not the enemy — but a good thing. Two whole nights in a row — and each time, the next morning, he slept in past 5:30 — once until 6:30 a.m. — I thought I was on vacation, and this morning until 7:00 a.m. I don't think I've been so rested in years.

Then tonight, he's forgotten how to sleep, and he's up and down, and fussy and squirmy, wants to be picked up, then does the Octopus Arms pushing against me until I set him down again, and then he cries to be picked up. How do you put an Octopus to bed?

It is comforting to think that at some point, we will ease into a routine, even for bedtime, and lullabies will sound, and Wuubys will be snuggled and we will all settle in for a long winter's sleep.

Secrets for a Mommy's Soul

This afternoon Ben asked me to come out and play in the back yard with him. I was putting the baby down for a nap and told him it would be a few minutes. He hollered as he walked out the back door, "I'll be waiting!" in a sing song voice.

He sat on the grass in the middle of the yard with a shovel and waited. I could see him from the window as I went about what I was doing, and he just kept sitting. Perhaps this doesn't sound as unusual to others as it is to me. My four-year old is *never* still. He is one giant mass of muscles because of how hard he plays — constantly. He climbs, he jumps, he swings from limb to limb on his jungle gym. I've caught him doing inverted crunches on his monkey bars. Not that he has any idea that he's doing an inverted crunch — he's just playing and he's probably pretending to be Spiderman at the moment.

So — anyway — once I got the baby down for his nap — I rushed outside to see what Benjamin was up to. He wanted to show me his various climbs, and then he wanted to hug me and tell me a secret. He wrapped his arms around me and in a husky little voice, he said, "I'm so lucky to be your son."

What made my little angel say such a lovely thing? Well — practice. Lots of practice.

It started a few months ago, and it started as my way to calm myself down when he was getting to me — when I'm frazzled and trying to do too much at once. I will breathe slowly in and remember that he's this little guy with his own little agenda. He's not seeing things like I'm seeing things. And most likely — he's not trying to get to me — he's just being this adorable kid with a lot of energy and a wild imagination. I will slow down long enough to very quietly say to him — "I'm so lucky to be your mom." Sometimes just slowing down and saying that sincerely is all I need to see a situation from the right perspective and keep my cool, even turn things around completely to be able to have fun again instead of butting heads.

Occasionally I get myself into a bad place and feel all woe is me for having so much to do, and so many people depending on me, and no time for myself, no down time, no alone time... yada yada yada. I need to remind myself how lucky I am to have these amazing people in my life — this amazing family — this amazing business that my husband and I are managing. We have a great, outrageous life. It's all in how we look at it. It's easy to feel overwhelmed — but much more manageable with the right attitude.

So — I get grateful for my kids — and that changes everything. And then the best part. They learn to check their attitudes and find gratitude also. They learn to cherish me back and tell me how lucky they are to have me. I can't think of a more fantastic thing for a mom to hear — EVER!

As Loud as my Fingers Can Snap!

"I love you as big as a house," we say. He loves us
"as big as a building that Spiderman would stand
on top of and swing from rope-to-rope-to-rope,"
and he's off — demonstrating the rope swing across the room
and down the hall, and somehow, he's forgotten
what he started saying. He loves us so much
that he forgets all about us to swing from
rope-to-rope through the house.

This is the love of a 4–year old. Until last night,
when he showed me that he loved me as much as he could stretch
his arms wide like a hug and then around his back;
basically, encompassing his whole known world — and that is
some
big love. Then he topped it off with, "I love you as loud as my
fingers
can snap" and proceeded to snap his fingers and nearly wake
the baby. That too is some mighty big love that made me cry.

As we start summer in a year when things are looking glum,
the economy is tanking, gas prices are hiking, natural disasters
are on the rise, and it's all starting to look a little apocalyptic;

doomsayers are in their element, it is up to us to stop the noise
and enjoy a summer splash in the kiddy pool with little ones
who cannot understand the fears of grown-ups. Take hints
from youngsters who see this as the time for ice-cream
and lollipops — for runs through sprinklers and fireworks at 4th
of July.

Let's barbeque with the best of them, and hold our friends
and families close — together we can weather this storm.
With big love and loud snaps, we can make it through anything!

This Much I Know

I would like to see how the waters
come down at Lodore* someday,
the words of the poet
skip and jump and leap and dance in my head,
rhythmic sounds, delicious descriptions
of tumultuous waters — perhaps every adjective
of the known world attached to that fall of water.
How I lapped it up as a child
requesting it beyond the point of pleasure for anyone else.

I realize children learn through repetition — I wanted
the same story every night for years. My boys will repeat
a phrase, repeat a picture they are drawing, repeat
an argument they create with one another.

There must be something comforting about the same
thing over and over and again and again. The patterns
forming security wrapped around their little hearts;
prone to wander, prone to stray, attached at my hip
through repetition, ritual and consistency.

They like to know what will happen next. What to expect.
They need to be able to trust that their lives
are somewhat predictable and secure.

They sing— song repeat things to quiet themselves
and guard against a scary, unsure world, what little
they know of the big world. And perhaps it's just
a Defense Against the Dark skill that will protect
them later — knowing how to make a pattern,
a ritual, a repeat. This I know. This much I know.

The waters come down at Lodore like before.
Stories come before songs before kisses before bed.
The sun will rise, and I am loved.
This much I know. This much I know.

*The Cataract of Lodore, by Robert Southey (1774-1843)

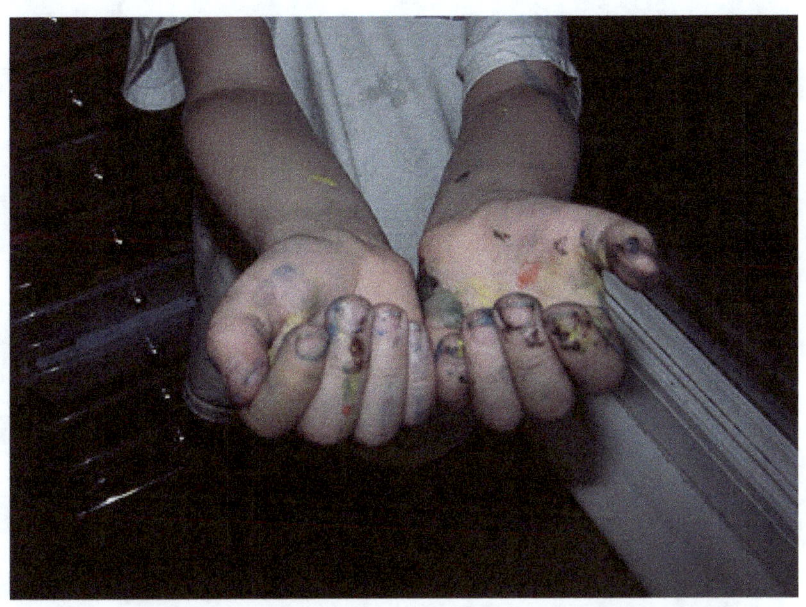

I was a Dark Storm Cloud

I was a dark storm cloud of a miserable mom yesterday after-noon. My little artist son has an artist's temperament, as do I, and sometimes those strong wills, and fierce emotions, and melo-drama collide, and we are a tangle of frustration with each other.

Luckily, we have been very clear about how dramatically we love one another — as big as the universe, as loud as the pipes on Daddy's motorcycle, as high as the sky, as blue as the ocean, as yellow as the sun. Our love has been described in so many ways back and forth — one day, Ben told me he loved me as much as all my shoes — and I have a lot of shoes. I love him as much as every blade of grass in the whole back yard — and we both agreed that would be nearly impos-sible to count. We have some mighty big love!

So — because we are so verbose and descriptive about our love, we are able to weather stormy days because one or the other of us will remember to say out loud — that "I love you even when I'm mad at you." And our dark and dramatic selves will have to smile and retreat a little and go create something of beauty together — because that's what artists do. We take our pain or our trauma and stir it together with all our dreams and wishes and spread all that stuff onto the canvas and smear it around until we forget that we started out mad.

Hot tears fall into the freshly cleaned commode

My hands are stuck inside my yellow rubber gloves;
scrubbing my bathroom with a vengeance.
Face hot, mind racing:
Am I not an artist?

I read about the demise of a friendship this morning;
"Now she's tied to a minivan," the poem said,
as if becoming a wife and mother
made the friend less desirable, relegated to
sad, frumpy housewife or soccer mom

and no longer worthwhile as a friend to art!
My toilet gets cleaned twice a week now;
as a young, bohemian artist living alone,
I doubt it got so much attention,
but today I have a house full of boys.

I'm the "Kool-aid Mom" I always dreamed I'd be;
that is, until my bohemian artist living alone period
when all I could think of was me or
what was wrong with the world for not noticing me?
I am proud to know these kids and watch them grow.

My seventh grader went to meet the Mayor
last year because I wanted him to know it's always
an option to visit someone important and tell him
what you think — He came out of the meeting feeling
like "A sixth grade legend!"

Exposing my kids to the world of literature and
reading aloud stories my parents read to me
that made me love books — isn't that raising another
generation of art lovers? Spaghetti finger-painting and
slurping noodles with the baby on his first birthday last night.

Am I not an artist? Am I not giving my family every
opportunity to experience life in creative, exuberant ways?
Staying up late to work on cut and paste poster projects,
or map projects or building a potato-launcher for a physics final.
Hot tears fall into the freshly cleaned commode,
Am I not an artist?

The Girl Drummer Band

She was just a slip of a thing, walking in slow motion between the towering musicians of her band, coming out from the stage door, taking her seat at the drums. She faced the crowd who were already mesmerized by her small, perfect arms, bared in a tank top, her mane of blond curls, and her steady gaze, completely sure of herself, ready to take us all on, ready to blow us away, ready to play.

She tore that place apart and broke a sweat, but it just glistened. She glowed. She never took her eyes off of us, we danced. We never took our eyes off of her, she raged on the drum set, full of rhythm and pounce, sure footed, sure fingered, hands and arms and back and neck, and those eyes, those eyes, they twinkled and smiled and even her laughing eyes pounded the skin of those drums. We loved her, the way she made us dance, the way she made us sure of our footing, sure of our swing, sure of the beat, and the pounding in our heads, and the song that we'd never heard before but could sing anyway because it was primal. We knew this music. We knew it in our arms, our feet and the hairs on the back of our necks that stood and danced along. This was the first dance, the way dancing ought to be.

This afternoon while driving home pounding out the beat of a favorite song on my steering wheel, full of joy and full of dance, I remembered the Girl Drummer Band and thought, if I could drum like that, I would always be in shape, I would never need to go to the gym. If I could just tear up a set of drums like that and burn up calories flinging myself all into my music, from rock and roll to praise songs to nothing but the drum and the sigh in between and the beat of my heart.

And I think what my life would be like with a drum set in the house. On top of the office that's already there, the teenagers, the toddler, my husband with his power tools, oh and the dogs, we get a second dog tomorrow night. Would there ever be a moment's quiet? Would I care? I start plotting how I can bring this about. This raucous, joyous madness that would be dance and laughter and if anyone had bothered to start it, dinner burning every night.

"The Turtles have Left the Building"

I call my husband to say this
triumphantly after an hour and a half
of getting ready. Everyone has
had an emergency or two — we've
all made several trips to the
bathroom — I have packed for
any possibility — and all along
the way I am trying to hurry.

After announcing that my
children are turtles — I drive
along wondering if I'm the
rabbit bouncing hither and thither
and getting less accomplished
than the slow and steady plodding,
exploring, and experiencing
of my little guys.

And it dawns on me that they
cannot rush
— and I need to slow down —
because they have so much

learning to do. As I am trying
my hardest to do something
quickly, they are getting caught
in imaginary swordplay with
a dining room chair and spinning
in slow motion to collide with
a wall, slither to the floor,
and melt into a puddle. This
is important stuff of which
neurons are built and the future
of our civilization depends.

As we drive, a flock of birds
is soaring over a pond — undulating
in great, sweeping arcs —
the sun glinting off their
wings and white underbellies.
They loop and shift in a
free-floating ballet.

I smile as I realize
that if the lead bird
in charge was task-oriented,
they would just fly
from Point A to Point B
with very little beauty.

As it is, they are not as
concerned with getting
there as they are with
enjoying the journey
and making the meandering

artful and elegant. This
they do naturally and with ease.

As I write, my son spins in circles
before me with a ribbon from
a present — it has been a jellyfish,
a cape, and a mask in the course
of the last few moments. What
a delightful way to live.
May I learn to tap into it
and make my meandering artful.

Wrestling with Night

My ninth grader will be reading "Night" by Elie Wiesel this year in his literature class at Clovis East High School.

I picked the book up months ago because it is also an Oprah Book Club selection. I got through about three pages before I was overcome with grief. I want to read it with him, because it is assigned reading. I have already purchased my own copies of every book on his reading list. But this one is so graphic. It is the story of a young boy who survived the Nazi concentration camps.

It hurts to even think of reading it, and yet I know how important it is. If we avoid the pain, we can accidentally forget. We must not forget. I sob just thinking of beginning. I'm sitting here right now wrestling with emotions. The thought popped into my head that I should try to be strong for my son. How on earth could I ever prepare myself to handle something so horrific? I cannot prepare. I just have to read it.

I've read other accounts, and just the knowledge of what was done is more than anyone can bear — but to read it with emotion attached, because the writer is brilliant, is an award winning writer, a Nobel Prize winner, and not just telling the facts — that is what scares me. It is a heart being ripped open before me, and I have to go watch and somehow participate in order to make sure we don't stand by and participate for real.

Fast forward a few days. I have now begun. My son has not. I needed to read it through on my own first to be able to know what was in store for us.

Teaching the bedtime routine

My own household's nights consist of our 2–year old learning to stay in bed once he is there. We are having to stay consistent and not just let him get up for one more snuggle, or one more glass of water. Otherwise our evening is chaotic with trips back and forth to the baby's room and not a moment to unwind until we go to bed.

But after I had read a chapter of amazing brutality toward children, my little one came creeping back into the living room. I welcomed the chance to hold him, to smother him with kisses. I couldn't hold back the tears as I cherished his little face. So many mothers during the Holocaust were deprived of this. So many parents had their children ripped from their arms. How could I not hold him every possible chance I get?

I am still struggling with wanting to protect my freshman son from having to read this. He was the one who, in sixth grade, decided that when he grew up, he wanted to be the next Abraham Lincoln or Martin Luther King Jr. He wanted to be significant in the fight against prejudice. I know that it is vitally important to remember what can happen when people forget to be human toward one another, when the world would rather not know the gruesome details because the details are disturbing. If we don't want to listen, horrendous things can be done because we turn our backs so as not to upset our stomachs.

My heart screams, "He's only a kid!" And then I remember that he's a kid who plays video games. While I sit here wanting to believe how innocent our children are — a surprising number of them are at their television screens blowing things up, shooting at people and witnessing conscience numbing violence.

I would love to say I don't allow this kind of thing. I try to put my foot down about the more graphic games, the ones rated for mature, but what I forbid might be easily available in other people's homes. These are signs of our times, and they frighten me.

Young shooters

It frightens me to think that children are now shooting people over minor irritations. A young girl in our Valley stood trial last summer for fatally shooting her mother and her mother's boyfriend because they told her to clean her room. This was reported in The Bee.

The girl had remorse after the fact, but at her moment of frustration, the most natural thing in the world to her was to aim a gun and pull the trigger. I grieve for her. Her conscience had been seared by a culture totally okay with violence.

I have just turned the corner in my own mind. I am now adamant that my son read this book. In fact, we should all read this book. Oprah is onto something. Our society is already condoning unbelievable violence. There is an old proverb which says that those who will not learn from history are doomed to repeat it. Our world is currently on the sidelines of another horrific genocide, this time in Africa. What will history say that we did to aid our fellow man?

Please join me in reading about one of the most gruesome periods of our history — not to revel in its brutality, but to avoid becoming part of it, to awaken our consciences and revolt against a tide that is bringing us closer and closer to accepting horrors like this as commonplace.

We need to be repulsed and spurred to action over tragedies, so that they cannot happen again. If the action we take is a real heart-to-heart talk with our kids about their video games, I will believe we may have a chance. If we go further and speak out to our policymakers about standing up for victims around the world, we will be even closer to being truly human.

This was originally published in the Fresno Bee,
Valley Voices section on November 18, 2006

Boomerangs for Sale!

And this is how we started our New Year. Scott and I were using the bobcat and the tractor to move dirt around since it was a lovely sunny day in Southern Oregon. We'd been moving dirt to the garden plot for over an hour, when I started wondering what my boys were doing inside. It was awfully quiet. Spells trouble. Who's hurting whom, I'm thinking. I'm just getting ready to go inside, when out they come with a bag of homemade Boomerangs, they're going to sell at the end of our Driveway for a Dollar each. (Made from tongue depressors)

As cute as their idea was — we couldn't let them be out at the driveway by themselves. What kinds of crazy parents would we be? The Doberman's were nearby, but foraging more than protecting, damn dogs. So, we took a couple pictures and then they put their stuff away.

But how adorable is their teamwork? So cute it almost makes me forget their darker moments.

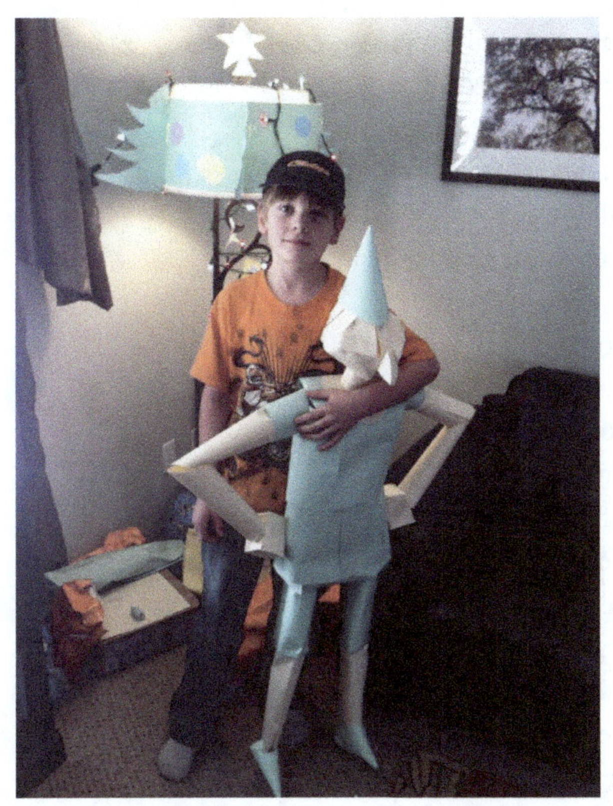

Christmas in Deep Freeze

For Christmas this last year,
my son built everyone gifts
out of paper and tape. We were
in the middle of a freeze storm
and trying to keep our animals
alive. We hadn't gotten busy
with decorating yet — so he took
matters into his own hands.
He made a paper tree out of a

lampshade on a tall lamp.
He made a life-sized elf to
greet us at the tree. He
made streamers and decorations
and multiple gifts for
each of us — each gift showing
an uncanny understanding
of the true nature of our
innermost desires. Gifts
truly from the heart!
My greatest gift — I think
ever — in my life — was
the paper open-mic night
he made for me with figures
that either sat on benches
in the audience or
could be moved to stand
on stage at the mic.
Out of paper. My heart
cut out into little figurines
and taped to a cardboard base.

"Do you like it?" he asked.
"Do you like it?" As I sat
sobbing, tears rolling
down my face. To be so
well-known and so loved
was almost too much to bear.

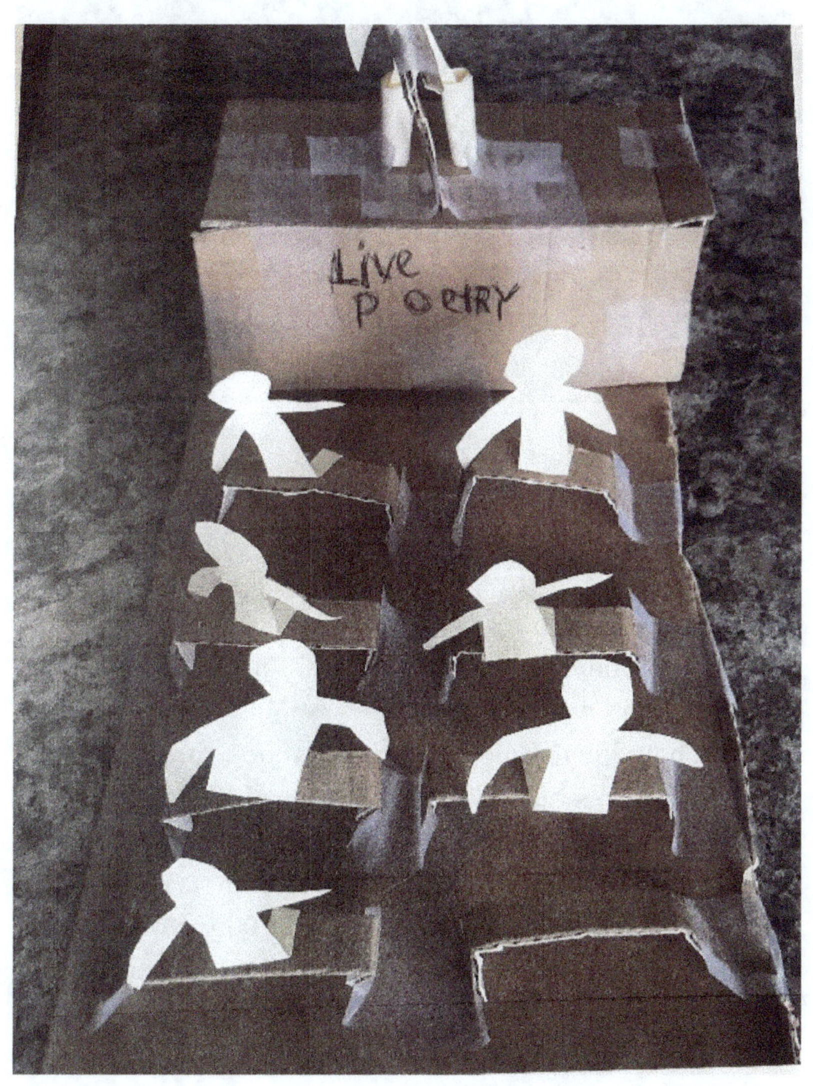
Live
Poetry

Say Yes

What would parenting be like if we used the Rules of Improvisation in our interactions with our kids? I'm not suggesting this entirely. I'm just wondering.

Right now, I'm reading Amy Poehler's book, "Yes Please." I've always liked her — but didn't know what a pivotal player she has been in the world of comedy. I didn't know that she was a part of the Upright Citizens Brigade and that they have multiple theatres and give classes (for $5) and trained 11,000 people last year, and, and, oh my word! No wonder she's sleep-deprived.

But in one spot, she shared the basic rules to be a great Improviser. She says you must:

    1. Listen

    2. Say Yes

    3. Support your partner

4. Be Specific

5. Be Honest

6. Find a game within the scene you can both play

My boys are comedians in the making, if I'd just get out of the way. They want to tell funny stories and get a reaction, and shock their listeners, and be hysterical. They want all that. Sometimes, they act like crazy people and embarrass me and I want them to stop, because I'm afraid they are making me look like a terrible parent, and I endeavor to shut them down or calm them down or stem the tide somehow of all the words pouring out of their mouths at high decibels.

They each had a friend over this last weekend, and one of the boys' moms hung out with me in the kitchen and drank tea as we began the process of getting to know each other since our kids are friends. When it was time to feed all the little hooligans a snack, my boys were cavorting and theatrical and it literally felt like I needed to apologize that we don't get out much, and all of a sudden, they had an audience, and all hell was breaking loose. They were fine. The other mom wasn't horrified, but I found myself wanting to tell them to Shhh, and tone it down, and eat their food and be quiet. I wasn't coming all the way out and saying that, but my hands were making little gestures, and wishing they would behave more respectably.

It's just that they WERE behaving exactly like a seven-year old and a ten-year old amped up because they have friends over would act.

So, I'm listening to this book on Audible, and when Amy Poehler gave the rules of Improv, something inside me jumped up and shouted and waved my hand in the air, and asked, "Can I do that as a Parent?" Can I just **Listen** and **Say Yes** and **Support my Partners** (kids) and **Be Specific** and **Honest** and **Find a Game**

within the Scene we can all Play? Can I do all that and have more fun, and stop shutting down their creativity because they get loud? What would it look like if I stopped trying to control everything and be in charge so much? I mean, I'm a parent, so I must be a little In Charge. I must provide some structure, balance, food and direction — but couldn't I grow as a person by allowing more Creative Play into our world, and spend less time trying to micro-manage them?

When I have these thoughts, part of me is concerned that I know so little about my job as a parent. Part of me is always fretting that I should be so much better at this, should know more, should be more confident in my decisions. Other people half my age, with younger children, are writing Parenting Books like they've got it all together. That boggles my mind. My kids keep changing and growing every single day, and it doesn't feel possible to keep up with them, let alone be a step ahead of them laying foundations for them and guiding them responsibly. No. I'm a flailing along and spluttering type of uncool mom, just trying every day to be somehow better at this.

I like the idea of trying some Improv Rules while Parenting. I looked that phrase up on Google to see if there are any books on the topic, any other moms experimenting with this, and Google didn't find a single thing. Perhaps this is a bad idea. Perhaps it's a fantastic idea, and I'm just the first one to have it. I feel like I should take a little bow.

Great and Simple Images
that Open our Hearts

"There's a great — with the significant risk of sounding a bit pretentious — there's a great Camus quote, in which he says something like, I may paraphrase, but, 'A man's work is nothing more or less than the slow trek to rediscover, through the detours of art, those two or three great and simple images in the presence of which his heart first opened.'"

— Sam Mendes, Director of the new James Bond movie,
Skyfall, in an interview on NPR this morning.

This quote almost brought tears to my eyes, especially perhaps, hearing it from a man. Hearing that men are always searching throughout their lives to rediscover the two or three great and simple images in the presence of which their hearts first opened. Wow.

What images are my sons seeing now, in childhood, which will move them to search high and low the rest of their lives for other experiences that will bring them the same thrill, the same soaring feeling as that first time their hearts opened?

And I know my sons have these enormous poet-warrior hearts, and I know they have seen beautiful, powerful images. I'm just wondering which ones are the ones that will be with them always, almost in a haunting way, just out of reach, just out of sight, over the next hill, around the next corner, pulling them, urging them out and onward for more?

We talk about planting seeds of love in our house. We talk about planting the things with our words and our actions that bring about the good we want to find in the world. We are artists. We talk about beauty and art and mathematics, even, and how these things can find the answers to the world's problems.

They love engines and motors, and speed. They love Iron-Man and Spider-Man. They are animal whisperers.

I'm so curious to know which of the two or three great and simple images are the ones that will (or have already) first opened my boys' hearts. I don't know that they will know at this age. We may have to wait and see and always wonder. It makes me feel even more passionate about sharing with them the great and simple things that have opened my heart.

And at the same time, in the back of my mind, all I can think about is The Grinch, and the moment his heart grew three sizes in one day. It may be as great and simple as that.

Oh, how I love this thought.

Superstar

I think it's safe to say
some of us just want to be noticed,
appreciated, praised for something,
acknowledged, cooed over perhaps,
a little adoring from the fans — name
recognition — just a smattering of
fleeting fame. (Some of us,
because I know my share of
introverts. This one will make
you cringe!)

Already, we have grade-schoolers
dreaming of the day their
video goes viral.

Last night, as I walked through
the grocery store on an errand
of desperation, because my
coffee cannot be restful or
refreshing in the morning without
Vanilla Creamer, I was spotted
by the Papparazzi — a holler
across the front of the store
from a Kindergartener. All eyes turned.

"Hey, you're Bean's mom,
aren't you?"

Pride filled my heart to be
associated in public
with that young, redheaded Superstar!

Constantly Knocking
Over the Teacups

I started to say that whenever we have a day where I feel like I've given my absolute best, I've poured everything I have into this mothering gig, and really done a bang up job, that's when my kids act out and get crazy and I end up becoming unraveled by bedtime... I started to say that, and then this story popped into my head.

The story of a guy looking for enlightenment, and climbing up a huge hill to meet with a guru, and telling the guru all the things he was trying to do to get enlightenment, and the guru started pouring a cup of tea, and continued pouring as the man kept talking. He kept pouring until it overflowed, and tea was everywhere. Finally, the guy looks at the guru like he's crazy. What the heck? Look at this mess. The guru says, "You must empty the cup to fill it. The cup is too full."

And I realize that my boys are my best possibility in life to ever learn serenity. Because as soon as I think I have any amount of cool, they go knocking over the teacups to give me something more to learn, to allow me to fill up again on what I need in that moment.

They are in constant motion, as I need to be to keep up with them. And this is not just a teacup we are trying to fill; this is our hearts and minds and souls. This family plan gives us a chance to learn all there is to know about love and understanding. So every time I think I'm doing so much for them and they should be grateful, yet they're acting out; I need to stop and think of all they are doing for me, and I should be grateful, and why do I want to act out? And maybe not so many shoulds. Maybe more grace. Maybe actually go pour a spot of tea and take some breaths.

I didn't quote anything from The Dude and The Zen Master — but I was reading it this morning when these thoughts occurred to me.

There Are Pillars

The four pillars of this and that,
the nine pillars of thus and such.
Some wisdoms have 13 pillars
and I am left not remembering
what any of them stand for,
but enjoying the view
from within my imaginary
pantheon — a walkway
of stone pillars lining
the covered stillness.
Blazing pink bougainvillea
climbing some, delicate
purple wisteria climbing others,
a white flower, perhaps
in the clematis family,
providing a little balance
between stark bright
and soft pale.

And I think of what I want
because life has become so much
more about all the things I need
to do and I've lost the little
child's voice who daydreamed

and wished whimsical about
my future. She had glorious
plans that included
leisure time — time to dream,
time to write, time to walk
and explore, time to stretch,
time to twirl, arms outstretched
in a meadow, time to skip.

Something happened along the way
and now I have long lists of
things to do, that are nowhere
near as fanciful as fingertips
touching the upturned faces
of flowers in a field as I spin.

I'm feeling quite grownup — in fact
closer to the end than to the
beginning. It seems to me
that the daydreaming to
become big has been shortchanged
by the Big Reality of being
grownup. And I wonder, truly,
if I can stop the world and get off
and find a way to fill my days
with wonder rather than worry.
Could I turn a switch like
that and focus instead on joy
instead of blasted practicality
and productivity and progress?

Is that just irresponsible or might
I find a secret passageway
to being a better mother
if I were somehow once again
a child or seeing through my
own child's eye, eye to eye
with all the wonder in the
world, big dreams, impossible
plans, wide eyed enthusiasm,
and crashing crazy tumbling
that are my boys?

I Have Been Waiting my Whole Entire Life for this Moment!

No, I cannot hide emotion well. I am a poet, for Pete's Sake. I feel everything deeply, I express what I feel in words or with tears, or with a face that says it all. I am easily read by those around me.

My little Bean is old enough to want to read The Chronicles of Narnia out loud with me, and I am beside myself with joy. I grew up in a Narnia-loving family. When my husband-to-be met my parents for the first time, we sat at a coffee shop so they could get to know him, and one of the first questions they asked him was, "So, what are your thoughts on Narnia?" Then literally, they both had their elbows resting on the table, their chins resting on their knuckles, leaning forward, gazing into his eyes to hear his breathless answer.

Well, that was when they realized that I was marrying an opposite for real and true. Scott is not a reader; he likes to work with his hands. He builds things, he does things, he tinkers and takes apart and puts things back together again. I read.

When I was little, my parents always had lots of people in our home. They worked with students and military folks. We had up to 20 people for dinner on a regular basis. There was lively conversation, often about politics or philosophy, religion and the

deep questions. After dinner, my dad would tell everyone present that he was going to read to us kids for a little bit. He would say that they were welcome to stay and read with us, or they could go in the other room and have coffee and dessert and he would be with them shortly. For some reason, no one ever left the table. They would just stay and figure it wouldn't take long to get through a kids' story and then they could get back to theorizing and debating.

Especially if it was an incredibly deep and philosophical crowd, he would pull out a Narnia book and start reading. After each cliff-hanging chapter end, it would be the adults saying, "Oh, please one more chapter! Oh, please one more chapter!" One by one, my three sisters and I would fall asleep at the table, and mom would cart us off to bed. People might chip in and help clear the table, but there were also nights when after four hours of reading, the dishes would still be on the table, and all the adults would be fired up to keep reading until they finished the book.

We realized early that these books are not just for children. When we were all still living at home, every so often, we would spread the word that it was Narnia night at the Arensmeiers' (my maiden name). People would come over dressed in comfy clothes, because we all knew we were going to sit in front of the fire, reading, until the wee hours of the morning when we finished the story.

I have read all seven books of the Chronicles of Narnia repeatedly throughout my life. I always seem to find something new. There are parts that make me cry, no matter how many times I've read them. I've read them to every roommate I've ever had. Somehow, my husband has evaded the Narnia experience, until now! Now, both my 4—year old and my 8—year old are clamoring for more and more Narnia. Bean said last night that Narnia is his favorite book in the whole world. Boy after my own heart, I tell you.

The thing is Narnia is allegorical and heavily symbolic. There are allusions to God and a relationship with him throughout. I have come and gone in my appreciation of religion in my day, but I have never once lost my love for Aslan. (I have not ever lost my love for the God of my understanding — just for anything at all to do with organized religion.)

The stories of Narnia were my introduction into the idea of things mystic and powerful, magical, wise, beautiful and sometimes terrible. Everything I know of sacred and holy, everything I know of the idea of reverence comes from Narnia. This is what I know and feel. This is the language that speaks to me, that comforts my heart when the world around me makes no sense. Narnia is more real to me than half of what I know to be true. Part of me, perhaps, has never really grown up at all. And now my children are entering into this door in the wardrobe with me. Life may never be quite the same.

The Stories of our Lives

It all started with Harold & the Purple Crayon.
My youngest and I read the story together
in front of a blazing fire and he said
he wanted to have this book in his collection
someday when he grows up and moves out.
I told him he would need his own copy
because there are some books I will always
need to have on my bookshelf
for grandkids or Nostalgia. I will always need
Narnia prominently displayed, and Winnie the Pooh,
and Harry Potter. I will always need Dr. Seuss
and Richard Scarry. We started listing out favorites,
and I told him the stories of certain books
I'd grown up with, that when I had kids, I knew
we would need, and how I searched for them,
and found they were out of print,
and paid large sums of money to secure them.
And that turned into the relating of certain stories
of our lives that we could hear over and over
again on nights like tonight, when we sit snuggled
in front of a fireplace, reminiscing and remembering
our fondest times. "Tell us again about the time you..."
and we all hunker down to hear all the parts
we know by heart, but want to hear anyway because

the telling and the hearing and the holding on tight
to the edge of the sheets, if it's scary, or the sitting
on the edge of our seats, if it's suspenseful, are a part
of us. We know how it ends, we know every line
and the punchline or the resolution, but we are
tied up in the story of it, and the cadence or the
song and meter of it. The stories that bind our world
together and give it a foundation and a soft place
to land, or a sure place to come home to. The stories
of how mom and dad met, or the day we were born,
and all the adventure around who we are
in our family, and what we mean to our loved ones.
The tapestry created by all our stories combining,
and holding hands, and making us poetry
that moves and breathes and scribbles its own
heart's longing onto the page with Harold — little
orange crayon marks that tell the wistfulness
of one of my own children dreaming of creating
new worlds of imagination
right alongside this little toddler hero.

Here's to Hilarious Late-Night Snacking

We were out later last night than ever before, I'm pretty sure. Somehow after our afternoon chores, we ended up going out to our Goat Mentor's place — way over in Applegate. It is always a several hour adventure to get there, up the crazy bumpy driveway, deal with the pack of dogs, get to the barn, pick up supplies, hug Sue a few times, watch the boys ride Tonka Trucks down hills, and then drive all the way home.

It was dark by the time we left with a gift of three new baby chicks. It was already 8:30 as we were getting out the driveway. Ben and Bean started asking if we were going to have dinner. We had wanted to stop at a Taco Truck on the way there, and our favorite truck wasn't where we thought it would be. So, closer to 9:00, we were stopping at a Pizza Place in Medford for a very late-night dinner. Our whole schedule was shot already. The boys were kind of climbing the walls.

We ordered our pizza and an appetizer. We were so hungry by this point, that we were starting to be cranky with each other. I went up to find out if the appetizer would be coming out ahead of the pizza, and the staff looked confused. They always time it to come out at the same time, they said. No worries. That totally works too.

Why even call it an appetizer, Scott and I were wondering aloud. The boys wanted to know what appetizer meant. I told them that an appetizer usually comes out before the meal as sort of an Appetite Teaser — to wake up your appetite and let it know that even more good things are on their way.

Then I remembered the other fun phrase, Amuse-bouche, which is just a one-bite type of appetizer. Usually, it is something complimentary from the chef — and it is literally supposed to be something tiny and delicious that amuses the mouth and tells you that there are tremendously amazing things on their way to your plate and your mouth.

Of course, it's French, and it sounds funny.

When our dinner arrived, both boys started taking little tiny bites, and giggling with each bite. A tiny laugh. A snort. A snicker. A hoot. That led to guffaws and outright hilarity. I couldn't stop laughing at them with their little gleams in their eyes — acting all French and proper, with their pinkies out, eating bite sized jokes and going on and on about how their food was so amusing!

The Resistance Will Speak French

The way that children solve problems
dire to the world is in whispers
on bunk beds or sketched across notebooks
with crayons and ideas and doodles
along the edge of the page for punctuation.
Thank goodness, they do not know
the enormity of the issues their
young hearts are earnestly addressing.

Their solutions in the quiet of the dark
make perfect sense according to the laws
of the playground and telling it like it is
that children are so good at — the
Emperor's New Clothes and all the politics
and double-speak that adults can
get subtly swayed by until they can
no longer see the truth — Children plow
right through that to laugh with open stares
at the nakedness and how far from grown-up
the grownups have become.

They have heard our discussions at the dinner
table and our requests for calm. They hear
messages in the play of children from families
with different outlooks — more vocal perhaps,
angrier, more ranting and more sound bites.

It jars my head and we keep trying to tell about
the good people working hard to
effect positive change — even if it
doesn't seem like that from the yelling
bits we see and hear.

Somehow — though I do not recall
making a big deal about the French Resistance,
somewhere in the stories we told, this little
spark landed on my youngest son's heart.

He decided that we should learn French
so we will be able to talk, and plan,
and shelter people right under the
noses of the bad guys when they come.

And they are building bug-out bags for
the Zombie Apocalypse because this is as
real a possibility to them as anything terrible
my husband and I might fear. They have their
cardboard armor and their swords of
aluminum foil. They are prepared to do battle
for us, and I pray with all my mother's heart
they will never have to.

So, we will learn the language of love
from a free class at the library and become
our own gorgeous force of opposition.

Pot. Kettle. Black.

Yesterday, I tuned into the radio just in time to hear the announcer say the title of the previous song, "Pot. Kettle. Black," and it stuck with me the rest of the day. The old saying wound itself through my thoughts all afternoon.

The point it kept making in my head was that there is not a better avenue for self-reflection and growth than being a mother/parent. I don't think any other experience in life gives us as many ways to see ourselves in the mirror and smooth our rough edges.

Every time one of my children is acting in a way, I think they need to change, I can see that they got that behavior from me. In some way, I have molded them, either directly by telling them and modeling for them the way they are to act, or by default, because when I'm not thinking, I act and model behaviors that they pick up way faster than the ones I intentionally want them to learn.

Oh, the tricky children!

I read a lot of mommy blogs, and I see a lot of rants. I have friends who are moms, and sisters. My whole world, it seems, is filled with other moms. The ones I gravitate to are the ones who are self-aware and patient with themselves and their children. The ones who are undergoing as much growth and realization as their children. I love to hear the things we learn from our own children. Yes, we are the ones who are responsible for teaching them, but oh, the things we learn along the way.

The ones who can't wait to get home and give their child a piece of their mind for some behavior exhibited at school, and share thrashing frustration of "I just don't know how to get through to him, I've tried everything," always give me pause. I see myself in that mode. I see myself mad and racing. And I know that those moments do not accomplish anything of lasting value. I learn from these moments too.

In these moments, I remember that absolutely everything about my children has a core and a beginning in me. There is a tether to me still. As they grow, and move away from me, they will take on things they discover in the big outside world, and their personalities will take on aspects all their own. At this phase, while they are under my care and in my home, if there are habits that need to be redirected, I need to first look at my own. Every hard edge that displays in my kids is a place I need to soften in me.

This is the most amazing therapy in the world: to have this much impact on another, and know that to guide my children well, I need to guide myself into the best, most gracious, most lovely paths I know to tread.

The photo of a black pot overflowing with a fountain of water, and nourishing gorgeous flowers, is an image I want to carry with me as a mother. Continuously, I pour myself out for my kids and nourish them as I remember to nourish myself.

This May Backfire

Every day in some way
I am chipping away
at their will to rebel in a surly way.
I have made rebellion
so utterly normal,
so quintessentially
human and natural,
so accepted and admired
even, I may just have
taken all the teenaged
go-against-my-mom
Shine off it. They know I adore
rebels, study rebels,
see a bit of the rebel in
every great work of art,
in every change to
society that was needed
and moved us forward.
In every shift in
consciousness that
brought new ways of
thinking, a rebel
was at the helm. Every great
adventure or invention

was because a rebel
was tired of doing things
in the ordinary
way and spread wings
and broke down established
modes of thinking and
ushered in something
entirely other and radiant.
Splendid and brilliant are
the ways of rabble-rousers
and visionaries. This may
backfire. I may have
unintentionally gone
too far and made rebel
something to aspire to
and perhaps that's not
entirely wrong. If seeing
rebellion — for my young
sons — creates an urge
to think and reason and
challenge the status quo
and break out beyond what
they see as every day
and the way it's always been,
and go out to the outer reaches
of their imaginations and
gasp in the places where
the air is thin, where thoughts
blaze and make their hearts
pound. My sons speak to me like,
"Dude, Mom!" They know if they ever
start acting out, I will be so honed

in on them, peeling back the layers
to see what box they are
fighting against, what bland
they are wanting to destroy.
I will be so with them
and for them and in their corner
encouraging their rebellion.
They know this. It is no longer
something they would do
against me and all my momdom.
It would be something
they would do with my full support
and we would crash through
whatever barrier was pushing
against them together.
God — I can't wait for my boys
to rebel. Is it sad that
I'll be sad if they don't?

You are All This
and Then Some

You don't need to wonder
or wish — you already Are
Something More. In so many
ways and in all directions at once.
You are magic and miracles,
you are a kaleidoscope of
impossible, beautiful,
rolled up into one wondrous You.

Why would anyone sift through
the diamond dust of you
to find the one pebble flaw?
Why focus on that rock — that
misfit thing? The cranky attitude
at breakfast, the doesn't wake up
well, the snaps at family. These
are pests and nothingness.

These are disproportionately
lectured on topics — these are
nitpicked and magnified
until the You of you — the

essence becomes minimized,
diminished, reduced to crumbs.

I remember being smaller than
a breadbox — only a collection of flaws.
I remember hunched shoulders,
mumbled words, non-words,
grunts and shrugs in response
to the implausible question:

"What is Wrong with You?"

Who knew — probably everything?
When NO — when Tiny overshadowed
all the rest — and unrest
at the edge of sunset.
Long darkness running far and away
over curbs and grass and drive
and road, up over swing sets,
a long, long dark Not Good.

How long I saw my shadow
as my evil, my inherent wrongness,
eyes downward, my whole spirit
a cave, a grotto, something grotesque.

I was a teenager once.

Inside with a candle,
my own little world, my own little
insights, and whispers and trying
to find beauty in brokenness,

my poet heart magnifying
the tiny bits of worth I could scrape
together into something I could hold.
A weed, a wreckage growing
between rocks and I sighed
and loved that relentless brave
thing that would stop at nothing
to shine it's ridiculous, microscopic
singsong into my dark and grey.

And I cannot help but see from the
other side now — that parents play
a part. When did I become a grownup
so easily focused on *Not*
what you want so much
to show?

You are all these great things
And then some!

Mothers

The conflict happens because she's right and she loves you.
And yet, we strive against all her rightness, her great ideas,
her prodding us into things that challenge and define us.

She made memories for us, with the books she read us,
the games she played, the places she took us,
the worlds she opened up to us,
the things she made it possible for us to believe we could do.

And when we hit brick walls, because our world and our emotions
were tumbling down around us, she stood tall
offering help and suggestions
we weren't ready to accept.

Her hand was always there to lead us across troubled waters,
or beneath a gorgeous waterfall — pulling us back
from a cliff, and we didn't want help just then.
We wanted to show how grown up we were,
how ready to fly.

And we strained against and fought and stormed
and stomped up to and over the edge at times —
into free fall and collapse,
all broken and bent and crushed
and destroyed at the bottom of some infernal ditch.

And now, as a mother myself, I can finally fully grasp
how desperately she wanted to help. How much she suffered
when I fled to do it my way, the hard way, because
her grown thoughts, her bright mind and life experience
didn't fit on my stubborn shoulders.

I knew more, and so will my own. And hold back
I will have to — as she did, and watch from afar,
because I won't be welcome in their turmoil.
I'll have so much to offer, so much to say.
so many ways to save them from themselves
and I'll have to console myself that eventually,
even the most wayward and strong-willed will remember,
will turn some corner, and think they've figured
it out for themselves,
the lessons I've been laying at their feet
all this time.

Brains on Fire

I have read that teenagers' brains
want to learn through hunger, thirst, and desire.
This is not something they do on purpose
to annoy us. They are chemically altered
because of their age and the enormous amounts
of growing going on in their brains.
They are drawn to things
that require everything of them.
They are tugged by sacrifice and meaning.

They do not even know this is happening.
They are pulled with a force they do not understand,
to crawl and scrape and hang from their knuckles
to get in at that window. They will not remember this
in the morning. They will not be the same person
tomorrow. Worlds are collapsing around them,
and being forged at the same time. Everything
is all or nothing, or who cares?

I remember so little of my youth, except the hunger,
and the longing for something other than what I had.
I remember drama for days, and not wanting it,
but not being able to escape it. I yearned for belonging,
for being someone's everything, anyone's anything,
just not me, here, alone with this brain on fire. Please.

I was given many rules, and narrow paths to tread,
and failure was inevitable. Shame and loathing
followed shortly thereafter, followed by screw it,
and indulgence at an escalated level for a very long time.

As a mother, I try everything to keep from pushing
my kids into rebellion. There are hardly any rules, and
wide paths, much freedom to express, be and be happy,
eat plenty of good food, read great books,
Play games, wrestle, explore, create.
All I want is for them to be happy, so I have
a teenager who rebels sometimes by hating everything.

Because Rebellion isn't a choice either, it is
hardwired obstinacy and required contrariness.
It is distancing me from you, to create a me

I can call my own. And I have to question everything.
I have to rip apart this fabric you have created
because I want to see the threads,
and Does the Center Hold?
And will you still love me however far I push you?

This is the balancing act of motherhood, remembering
enough of my own defiance to trust
my children to wage their battles fiercely,
to come into themselves in all their glory.

STAY

The hearts and souls of them
and me and mine collide
and spin and splatter
some DAYS
when the muse is heavy
and I long for solitude
to weave myself into
lines on the page
to drift and LAZE
to melt and roam
through images
and loaf after a thought,
an idea, an odd recollection,
pull memories from the HAZE.

They want ALL of me,
all my attention
my curiosity
devotion
my wonder and PRAISE.
And I want to give it,
these children with
their imaginations
their stories and plans

big dreams and creations
their futures all
possibility in BLAZE.

I am wrapped up
in marvel at them
at every turn,
every spin, dance and fury
each explosion of new
ideas, new developments
or creative PHASE.

And I am torn,
pushed and pulled,
thoughts and half words
splutter out before
I can disentangle
and get myself to the PAGE.

Not every poet should
be a mother. I've read of
manic moments and meltdowns,
pulled too tight, and taut and snap,
the tension between want
and need, duty and desire
all jumbled in a CRAZE.

The struggle for balance
Atlas Shoulders bent low
to carry all their world.
We stumble over teardrops
and punctuation

and our own matter WEIGHS
us to crumbles, to broken
and flattened if we focus
on wanting and lack,
if we think back to hours
of free time to write and ponder
before having a keeper of DAYS.
Bean minds our calendar
and X's out the blocks
and counts down to the next
big event or HOLIDAY.

Time will slip through
our cupped hands, our
too firm a grip, our clench
and our grit, and our SPLAYED
out to make outlines
for Turkey art.

Before we know it — we
will have old hands
full of wrinkles, our finally
quiet house will be deafening,
as we long for their sounds
through the house,
their endless PLAYS.

My own mother
warned me not to
yearn too much for
time to write — "Your
children are the Poems

You are Writing
during this Time," she said,
as these
moments will quickly
dwindle until they STRAY

Far from home and busy
building castles in the air
and I will once more have time
to long for and long for
recreating moments
out of fragments
recapturing and wishing
I'd spent more time
asking them to STAY.

SECTION FOUR:

A POET PEEKS OUT
AT THE WORLD

Days of Soup & Holler

It seems as if the geese could
bump into each other in this mist,
each screeching into the void
sounding out to the others
calling the way forward
southward, onward toward the
next season, the next warm nest.

I can't see to the end of my driveway,
fog hanging in white, billowing curtains,
pulling me into the story,
some elegant myth, where rooms
are always long and tall and
sparsely furnished, but for the
draperies blowing in from the veranda.

And I, out standing in my field,
in layers of scarves, for the same effect,
hair blowing; it's so romantic,
except for the bucket of hog mash
I carry, and the muck boots
that keep me grounded so I
do not gracefully float
from one chore to the next.

The wild geese are squawking
in their dramatic, it's the end
of the world way — which is
how geese sound all the time,
not just when they can't see
the path ahead of them; my own
geese are always at their wits
end over the trauma of waddling
across their yard
to get food from my hand.

Their cries in the grey, leading
others to follow, their beacons
of sound and "We are in this
together," remind me of
the place in my heart that gets
knit together at the sound of
another's words, an honest howl,
a sigh, a shudder, a tear
that resonates with me, speaks
my whole world in a teaspoon,
and I cannot always see beyond
my own feet, my own muck and mire,
but I know there are others ahead
out there in the mist, the fog so thick,
I won't say it,
I will not say it,
It resembles pea soup not one bit.
What crazy whimsy
would see this as green?

Ahead, pushing through panels of white,
gauzy stage wrap, lost in layers,
trying to find the opening
to give a bow or start the narration,
is someone just like me,
struggling, and putting on a smile
because here are the lights,
and here is the show,
and we've forgotten our lines,
we'll make it up as we go.

A $68.9 Million Dollar Modigliani Painting and A Homeless Man

Nov. 3, 2010...**Modigliani's $68.9 Million Woman Auctioned At Sotheby's** — creates a record-breaking sale to start off the Fall Art Auction season.

When this hit the news just last week, the first person that flashed across my mind was a homeless man in San Rafael. He could have been a Shakespearean Actor; he had such bearing and poise. He was extremely focused on ritual. He moved in set patterns around Marin County, just across the Golden Gate Bridge from San Francisco. He would stand on a street corner across from the building where I worked in downtown San Rafael and hold court.

He would go shirtless in the summers and display a well-honed and crafted ebony physique. He wore a rag on his head. He spoke like an itinerant preacher, belligerent orator, and professor-at-large, eloquent and unintelligible at the same time. He clearly had cycles of delirium, or medication, where on every third day, he would be lucid and be able to form clear sentences. The other days he would rant and rave, arms flailing, impassioned speech, just without any real point per se. Sometimes he would gather a crowd of onlookers, trying to decipher his speech.

At other times, he looked like a dangerous crazy person, and passersby would creep to the other side of the street to avoid him.

On the occasional days when he was in his right mind, he would join me on the stone benches in the shade at the Bank of America building where I would have my lunch and read. At first, he frightened me a little. But I came to know him as harmless to me, and interesting. Fragments of conversations were all I was ever able to have with him. I never could get his name, I would ask, and he would get distracted by something and go off on a tangent. He wasn't even on his best days completely cogent.

However, he complimented me, and what girl in her early twenties doesn't want to hear something lovely spoken of her? In my early twenties, my best physical features were more prominent than perhaps they are in my forties. I had long legs, a long neck and my red hair was much more vibrant in those days. He would call out to me, mid-rant from across the street even, and refer to me as "Legs." That, alone, could be seen as objectifying, but remember, I was twenty and was rather proud of my long legs. But he also called me a Modigliani Girl. He would draw attention to me, as if the people wandering by quickly trying to get past him were his actual audience, glued to his every word, and he would tell them about me, that I was exactly the type of woman Modigliani loved to paint.

I had to look the painter up, and back then, I don't think the internet was quite what it is today. I had to go to a Library to look up what kind of woman this made me. From what I could gather, Modigliani was one of those brooding, alcoholic artists, who squandered his talents and tortured his creativity with self-medication and drug induced deliriums. He died a pauper and his wife jumped out the window killing herself and her unborn child at the news of his death. It didn't sound like a compliment by any means to be associated with this dark artist. But I also saw that he painted elongated forms, long necks, long torsos, and ballerina-like long legs. Whether his models looked like this or not, he seemed to always see long, elegant shapes.

This fascinated me. I wondered about this homeless man and his knowledge of the art-world. I wondered if he himself was some sort of tortured artist, or simply a lover of art. Perhaps, art has always been how I relate to others, whatever their station in life, whether we have anything else in common or not, I find ways to discuss art, or the artist's way, the need to create, the desire to communicate with others in some way, the ability to see beauty in tragic figures, the sixth sense that everything is connected, that all matter is here to be formed somehow into something beautiful.

Several years passed, and I was working in Sausalito. I walked outside my office, and there in front of the Safeway, was a tall, stately street-man with a rag on his head, seated, relaxed, and resting against the wall as if he was in one of his calmer days. He looked up and quietly said, "It's the Modigliani girl!" I smiled and shook his warm hand, and tears came into my eyes, that he would remember me.

Today, I wonder where he is, and if in any way, he is still a lover of arts, a soap-box speaker on a corner, enlightening people to the ways of the world, and pointing out what he thinks is beautiful to everyone who passes his way. I wonder if he knows that the artist who died alone and miserable and poor, just had a painting auctioned off for millions of dollars. Perhaps he only ever pretended to be crazy. Perhaps he bought it for himself.

All this Talk of Rosemary
and Religion

There is nothing like the smell of fresh Rosemary,
fresh between fingers, fresh from the garden,
dirt under nails from digging, dirt on knees;
you could say from praying, but it isn't, really.
Unless praying is *cooing* to the plants
doing well, inhaling deep to fill the lungs,
and knowing each miracle of bud unfurled
is another occasion for wonder.
Worn, green fingers smell of tomato plants,
mix with herbs, mix with dirt,
now mix with sun rising and birds beginning
to chatter. We have so much to remember.
We have too much to forget.
We have forgotten how to be simple,

how to act justly, and love mercy,
and walk humbly with our God.*
The trickle of water to tender plants,
the buzz of helpful bees.
These things are holy windows
beneath cathedral skies.

* Biblical reference — Micah 6:8

Ferocious Calm

I am angry and I feel slighted and I'm aware this is childish,
but I want to pout and stamp my foot and behave inappropriately.
At the same time, I know this is beneath me,
that I can and should rise above, the issue at hand
is of no consequence. I was literally upset over nothing,
a minor inconvenience, but my pride was hurt.

Even if the issue was something grand — as there are
many grand outrages unfurling around me.
There is a part of me that knows:
There IS a decent way to behave,
there IS a noble high ground.
There Can be substance in a debate
regardless of the behavior of others.

I can hold myself accountable.
It is my responsibility to keep myself
from becoming completely unhinged
and baring my fangs to the world.

In a world increasingly set on automatic Boil-Over,
where grown-ups are fist fighting in Parliament,
where leaders and politicians are physically attacking;
our civic dialogue has degenerated to drunken brawl behavior.

It would be so easy to jump in and stoop to that level.
Because even at that stage, someone with a vocabulary
could be fierce, could dominate, could overpower.
But inside, there is a place of fighting calm,
a place resistant to aggression.

There is a pool of serenity, and the waters are troubled.
There is quaking and furrowing of brows,
there are pensive lips, there is a storm of uncertainty.
And then the realization that this is the beauty
and the challenge of spiritual growth. As uncomfortable
as this feels — this struggle; the wrestling between
what we feel and how we want to feel,
how we know how we would like to address this issue;
all the while having our wayward inner child
screeching and frothing at the mouth.

To Know there is a better way is half the battle.
To have a compass pointing toward the path
of the soft answer, and the spirit cleansed
in the fires of love. It is not easy.
It is not sappy or pat answer. It is a ferocious calm
and a low, sustained, rumbling growl
from the throat of Aslan that keeps me,
that holds my words in check,
that guides my attitudes in times of trouble.

And I am not strong in Peace.
I am still clawing my way up that wall,
but my solace is that I know where I stand
in the midst of the turbulence.
I am a beginner at this transcendent stuff,

a novice, a tiny grasshopper — but there are seeds of love
that have been planted, there is discipline being learned.
I stand with love and growing up.
Eventually, I may even have the self-control,
the wisdom, the sense
to do in every situation exactly what is needed.

Metronome

The blades on the windshield wiper
swish back and forth, as rain
pelts down in gusts — fast and hard,
then slow and steady and all the while
the blades shift left and right and side to side.

The secondhand ticks in increments
around the face of the clock, not
missing a beat as the day slowly dawns,
sun shining on each blade of moist grass,
birds singing and early risers sipping coffee.

The day picks up speed, it seems, as kids
wake up and the noise level escalates,
but sure as the sun rises in the east,
the second hand keeps its steady tock
through every high and low of activity.

Perhaps the ups and downs, the heights of joy
and despairing valleys we feel are simply the
metronome of life keeping time to the symphony
of our days — a steady tick tock, back and forth
marching out a beat to keep the music fluid.

No matter how raucous and vibrant, or achingly
poignant the melody becomes — there is
a rhythm at the base of it all, a beat that ties
each stanza together and melds the highs and lows
into a richness and depth of beauty
no pain-free life could accomplish.

Braille Bible

Last week, I sat next to a woman
with a Braille Bible. At her instigation,
I felt the page — and ran my fingers
along a line of scripture, and touched
a cord — deep pangs of longing.

My eyes have seen, my heart
has swelled, but oh, to have that physical
connection — to have God's words
travel from my fingertips
through my nerve endings, my hands,
my arms, to my very core — to feel it
in my heart, my head, my body.

The page is completely white;
no embellishments or decorations —
no fancy sidebars — just the Word.
To experience the Word made flesh
with fingers of flesh, the sense of touch;
to see His face with fingertips.

If it is possible, the page was a blur
before me as tears welled up to blind me.
I cherish my sight but envy her vision.

Hallelujah

It comes on and I sing along.
It pours out its heart, it's a
cold and it's a broken
Hallelujah.
And it's so easy to sing,
so much like a hymn,
so much like a praise song,
but Not.
It is worshipful, reverence
and loss, it is NOT Anymore,
it is Gone, It Once Was.
It once cared. It once was a place
to call Home. It once Nourished
and fed and beckoned and belonged.
It once Taught and Instructed.
It once provided Hope and
Assurance. For a time,
We might have been Saved.

Until it became Cold and Broken
or hollow. Until we saw
through to another side,
the smoke and the mirrors,
the Terribly Human,

the Fall from Grace,
the Feet of Clay.

But it is one of those deliciously covered
songs in Rock and Roll,
leading me to think
many of us grew up in church pews.

There is a longing for some of it
to be real — we linger over
this song, the phrasing,
the haunting melody and our lips
caress Hallelujah
over and over again
in quiet reverie
for what once was
Something Sacred.

She Thought Perhaps Azalea

4/29/15 As Baltimore was burning

My troubles are so damn small
in comparison to cities burning;
they are not the world's troubles
like the anger, anguish
and outrage bursting
from the inside out
of our cities and our towns,
our neighborhoods broken,
our people destroyed.

And as much as I want
to claim them as mine
to feel a solidarity,
I know I am a pale outsider.

Sitting on a bench at the playground
next to a beautiful brown mama
and her precious, brown baby boy,
tears welled up in my eyes:
the weight of my privilege
too much to carry today.
Wanting too much to seem casual,

I glanced out at the green grass,
sun-dappled through enormous, beautiful trees,
the pink and white flowering bushes.
"Do you know their names?" I ask.
"Are those Rhododendron?
I can never be sure."
She thought perhaps Azalea.

She saw my tear-filled eyes,
and I gulped, and mused
at the beauty all around us.
I could not ask a total stranger
How to talk
about Race in America today.
I just sat on the bench with her
and adored her little son,
and breathed in and breathed out
and tried to will our world to do better.

She laughed at my boys and their antics.
We had the common ground of motherhood,
which I'd always thought could not be underrated;
but see that I will never
have to worry over mine
in anywhere near the same way
as she will worry for hers.

I kept wanting an entry into conversation
that would give me the chance to prove
my worthiness as a non-hater,
that would give me a reason
to enumerate my encounters with hatred,

with me and my black friends on
this side, or list my affiliations,
the amazing men and women
who I have considered friends, roommates,
Family. But there was no segue
from clapping, chubby baby hands
to any deeper issues. And my brushes
with color do not give me,
do not begin to give me...

I only know the outsiders anthem,
I do not carry inside me the root,
the flower, the core. The baseline
of this descent, the chorus through
the ages, through the cages,
through the caged and chained,
the families broken,
The stand-up tall — no matter,
The don't cry — does not matter,
The run, the hide.

I never knew run.

I have never known hide,
nor life or death;
no one to trust.
I talk to cops, I have flirted
my way out of tickets.
I know nothing.
I stand helpless on the outside
knowing f*ing nothing.
Knowing beautiful babies

Grow up to be target practice.
Shoot. Fire. Aim.
Think later.
Cover up.

Restored

Have you ever been in a real-life scene that takes on otherworldly proportions because of its simplicity and beauty? The other day, I beheld something so lovely, music should have been pouring over it to preserve it.

It could have been choreographed;
it could have been a dance
of intricate steps and weaves
and passes — pulled up close
then spun away. It was just
the grocery store after work.

Busy people — every lane full,
and no children crying,
no one huffing or distracted.
It was a symphony.
It was precision of checkers
and customers, big brothers
looking out for little brothers,
kids helping parents bag
produce. It was connection
and eye contact and small
pleasantries and people
working together.

It was a brilliant smile on a woman
as she joked with her cashier.
It was a renewed sense of faith
in humanity. There was no outrage
over politics, no seeing "Others"
as dangerous. It was busy
and humming along with
cordial strangers and a toy dropped
by a baby and picked up and
replaced by a hand that felt
the need. It was ordinary people
being extraordinary. It was a full feeling
of all is right with the world
in this tiny, precious moment.

It was people dressed for work
and going home as if they had
something waiting there for them:
a child to hug, a partner to enjoy,
a show to watch, a walk in the garden,
a long view from the back porch.
It was life and I got to feel it being
lovely.

It wrapped me up in warm thoughts
and tucked me in and
kissed my forehead.

The Beauty of a Strong, Silent Shoulder of Solace

And just like that, the other shoe drops. Sometimes right in the midst of a personal joy, we are encountered by a friend's sorrow, and what do we do? Yesterday I called a friend to tell her my big exciting news. I was actually bouncing around a little with enthusiasm for my big deal. She answered in a whisper, which right away told me this may not be a good time. She was in the I.C.U. with her sister-in-law, who had been in a terrible car accident and may not make it through the night.

Of course, my exciting news evaporated as I tried to reach through the phone cord to wrap my arms around her.

Because I always write about Beauty from perspectives that we wouldn't normally associate with Beauty, I thought today I would write about beauty in the face of tragedy. What is the most beautiful expression of concern you have ever experienced? Who stands out to you as a pillar of strength when your whole world was falling into pieces?

For me, it is my former roommate Gail, who sat with me one afternoon in silence as I cried to tragic sounding classical music played over and over again because that music spoke my heart in ways I couldn't muster words to speak. The music seemed to be giving me permission to feel the weight of my sorrow, and it wept along with me.

I was dealing with a loss of enormous proportions; the kind of loss that doesn't just heal up real quick and become easily forgotten. No. This was the kind of fragile situation that would be with me for the rest of my life, to varying degrees. Over time, the hurt maybe lessens, but it's always right there under the surface. All it takes is a look in that direction, and all sorts of feelings come up again. I was in the midst of *that* kind of hurt.

There was nothing anyone could say to make it better. No one could say, "Oh I know just how you feel," because it's not true. No one can know exactly how another person feels when that person is devastated.

Gail sat with me. She never said a thing. She didn't pat my head and say, "There, there," she didn't try to help me snap out of it or think of something happy. She didn't do anything at all to try to console me, and in not doing a thing, she gave me the greatest comfort anyone could have given me. She participated in my sorrow. I knew she heard me. I knew she felt along with me. And she gave me all the time I needed to cry until I couldn't cry anymore, and I was ready to go do something else. I will never forget what a gift she gave me.

My father is a minister and he has been with people in hospitals going through excruciating pain and loss. I remember the story he told me about when he was a young minister and he got a call that a family had just lost their young child. He rushed to the hospital to be with them, and before he entered their room, he prayed for words of comfort. Once he was there, he wrestled with what he felt was an appalling failure as their pastor, because no words whatsoever came to his mind. He struggled to come up with anything, just one comforting word. And the harder he tried to think of something, the more his mind was blank.

He sat with them for an hour and a half in silence. The entire time, he was waging battle in his heart to find what he felt they needed to hear from him. Finally, as he stood to leave, feeling like he had let them down tremendously, he reached for the mother's hand. She held onto him and through tears thanked him profusely. "For what?" he said incredulously. "For not saying *anything*," she responded. She told him that well-intentioned people had come to say that we are to be joyful in all circumstances (a scriptural reference) and that God always has a plan. She said that deep in her heart, she knew that, but at this moment, she just didn't want to hear it. It was the furthest thing from comfort.

My father said that this was the greatest lesson he could have received about being a good pastor and being with someone in a time of sorrow. Over and over again he has been with people in catastrophic situations where their worlds have suddenly been turned upside down. He has witnessed the well-intentioned, but cruel messages of hope people try to deliver. He has stood or sat beside people for hours on end as they wept, and been told repeatedly that he did more for them than anyone else, because he didn't try to say anything to make it better.

I think of my Dad, and I think of my roommate Gail and the enormous gift she gave me of being my friend, who silently sat with me, enveloping me in great swaths of solace without saying a word.

Rebels

Lately I've been wondering
about sacred texts and rebellion.

About the Big Questions of humankind,
the pounding conundrums
all down throughout time,
and the rebels that ushered in
new ways of thinking.

The ones who broke from
the known, the accepted as
The God's Honest Truth
and peeked around the curtain
and found something odd
or something beautiful
or nothing at all.

Who wrestled with angels,
or laughed in God's company;
who were bold enough to question
the status quo, or push the boundaries
of what we can acceptably
ask of our elders.

I've wondered about those who,
from an early age, resist labels,
or confined spaces, or
what we expect of them;
whose voices
are deep and dark and scary, or
who say nothing in answer to our questions,
but paint lavish scenes or doodle
brilliant geometries in the edges of their books,
who see things we don't,
hear things we cannot,
answer to a muse who demands
their finest in ways we do not comprehend.

I have wondered about rebels
because my children are teetering on the edge
of the teenage years and mine were fraught
with pining's for something other, off and away,
worlds apart from what is traditionally offered.
My daydreams took me elsewhere,
and I was urged to be real, and here, and now,
and toe the line, and do what I was told,
and I didn't want any part of that, thank you.

I found my voice screeching and screaming,
and raged and torn. Darkness had an allure,
with a heartbeat and a full throttle.

My questions were not out of order.
My hunger was completely
in line with who I was, who I am,
what makes me tick.

It did not suit my family.
It did not suit that story.

But I had stories of my own
and lifetimes of questions to ponder.

I have been wondering when
religion will stop pushing away their rebels.
Their rebels have often created something
good and closer to the truth.
Rebels sense the heart of God perhaps More
than the toe the line, ask no questions crowd.

When will it be acceptable to stare and wonder,
to delve the mysteries, and taste the sugar in the rind
of ache and swell, of love and loss and life?

The Painting that Broke
my Heart Wide Open

Why did this giant, yellow painting
split my heart wide open the way it did
and make me cry with wonder and love and
"I need to have this!" — with such intensity?

It is full of hope in shades of
barbed wire.
Small cross hairs across the expanse,
and they could be fence spikes
or stars.
They could be nonchalant,
just marks at specific intervals,
or they could be counting moments
in an hourglass.

It sings joy to me.
It sings joy.
It sings.

It was meant for me — I am convinced.

I walked around a corner
at a gallery and spotted it
and burst into tears.
Someone pointed out the artist
and I went to him with my eyes
still misty and a catch in my throat,
and thanked him for making something
so beautiful, so heart-stopping,
and then I was overcome again
and couldn't speak — for the tears.

"Oh, come here, and give me a hug,"
he cried. He'd never moved
anyone to tears before,
he told me later.

Yellow is the color of healing.
A woman at the gallery asked if
maybe something in a previous life
was calling to me from this painting.
Yes!
My young-adult life was fraught
with loss and pain and tragedy —
generally staged by my own
poor choices. My early poetry
was all about trying to heal broken
parts of me. Now I don't feel
broken. I feel vibrant and joyful.

This painting reminds me of my
journey to joy, my journey
through pain, my hope appearing,
my dogged determination to
see silver linings,
my heart lush and rolling
with gratitude for
the life I have today.

Permission to use this photo of the artist's work has been granted
by the artist, John Lambie.

SECTION FIVE:

FINDING HOME IN A
COMMUNITY OF WRITERS

Poem to Young Poets

I am a grown woman
with children and grandchildren
You are but a child and yet
I would sit at your feet
and be a student
of the way you form words
into raw emotion
Chills going up and down
my spine
Tears streaming
from my eyes
because your story
is so powerful
and you speak with
such authority
Your silence
splits   rocks   open
in the pauses between
words
Every breath
is metered
to bring the most
impact
You are precision

and vision
You are righteous
indignation
and a mighty choir
bursting forth
from your tiny frame
You are a young Poet
and I envy you
I am in awe of you
I want to study you
behold you
and watch you transcend
and transform
become and radiate
usher in the life
you will create
the world you will reshape
I am a student
I will sit at your feet
and drink in all
that you are able
to share with me
I am your audience
I am your cheering crowd
I am your fingers snapping
heads nodding
feet stomping
in raucous approval
I am listening with all my heart
I am your paper
I am your pen
Write your words

across my spirit
Etch your manifesto
on the windows
of my soul
Break my heart
Rebuild my tower
I stand taller
knowing you speak
knowing nothing
could make you
be silent
Whatever this world
feeds you
You will turn to verse
and we will all
be saved by the
truth you speak
the truth you dare
the truth you share
the truth you are
what slices through you
this sword in your hand!

As Trees are Born
to Bear Leaves

I am sure that some are born to write as trees are born to bear leaves: for these, writing is a necessary mode of their own development. If the impulse to write survives the hope of success, then one is among these. If not, then the impulse was at best only pardonable vanity, and it will certainly disappear when the hope is withdrawn.

C.S. Lewis to Arthur Greeves,
The Letters of C.S. Lewis, (28 August 1930)

Today I read a question: What is your Spiritual Practice? from Amy Putkonen over at Tao Te Ching Daily. What is the thing we go back to over and over again that brings us peace and comfort and a connection to what we find sacred?

For me it is writing. I have always written. There have been times when the longing to be published, that pardonable vanity, was so strong, that I hurt for lack of an audience. I wanted to share my thoughts and feelings on a grand scale and get a response. I wanted more than a monologue, I wanted a shared experience, a dialogue, a give and take, applause. And the roaring of those yearnings almost drowned out the need to put words on paper in the first place. I have been disheartened, and discouraged, looking at younger writers with an already enormous readership. I have thrown my pen at a wall. I have decided to give up writing.

I have suffered from the distance I put between myself and a blank page.

This is in me. This is my spiritual practice, where I work out my issues. When I am hurt, I go to the page. When I am delighted, I want to capture the moment on paper. When I am in love, I overflow with more words than my beloved can handle, and I take some of it to the page. When I struggle, to the page. When I wonder, to the page. When I am lost, to the page I go, again and again, and I find myself at the feet of the Divine, and I sink into the earth to worship.

Sometimes it has been poetry. Mostly, it has been poetic wanderings, not necessarily technical poems, but my world view from a poetic standpoint. What I see through that lens. How I try to be a better mother by seeing my children poetically, or seeing them as poems in the making, or poems too perfect to alter.

It has hardly ever happened that I thought something brilliant and decided to go write that down. Generally, if I write something that floors me, it spills onto the page in an outpouring of emotion and words and euphoria that I don't even understand. I take a breath and reread and realize that something wonderful just happened, and I was a part of it somehow, and there are those words, in that order, in that phrase, and I want to wrap myself in them and surround myself with them.

This is my spiritual practice. This wordplay; this moment in front of a blank page, the quiet before, and the breathlessness after. The will to fill it. And then the running out and tackling a friend to hear it.

My Poet Heart

This morning as I listened to Flamenco Guitar music on my way to work, the thought exploded in my mind that the reason I am a poet is because I'm a scattered mess of an artist. I don't think all poets are this way; I am not at all speaking for anyone else.

All I'm saying is that there are so many things that I love that I would gobble up and devour, if I could, if it were possible to ingest every style of music simultaneously, I believe I might try. I have no idea how to dabble in art, realistically. I want to paint murals, sing from a rooftop, write a symphony, play every instrument with passion and conviction, pour myself into a dance that tells a story and breaks my heart, leaves me breathless at the end, and leaves the audience in tears.

I want to take a soul-satisfying long drawn-out drink of a cello; I want to drink like I'm in a desert and this instrument is my one chance to be whole again. I love the cello, I adore the violin, the piano makes me well up I love it so much.

And the compositions themselves, and the composers: I love them all. I love the stories behind the music, the irrational fears that become music and racing hearts and dancing and leaping into the arms of a beloved. I love the artists who chop off their own ears, for who knows why, but all the thoughts and dreams and creative inspirations burning through their brains and shooting like sparks from their fingertips, keeping them up at night, who knows if any of them ever sleep, I love them all. I have artistic children. I know from a small distance what goes into artist's heart's; all the love, all the ingenuity, all the mile-high dreams and concoctions that can spin them dizzy.

If I could, I would embrace every form of art and create a cocoon of bliss for myself. Instead, one by one, piece by piece, I try to share in words what is more beautiful than I can sometimes fathom, what seems to be beyond mere words' ability to express. That is the quest of the poet, to put in words, what leaves lovers of beauty speechless.

This is what I love about poets — their enormous grasp, their endless ability to mystify. This is why I am a poet — if I could consider myself in their realm, I would reach and grasp, I would leap with my heart in my hands to crouch before you, and with eyes tear-glistened and wide with wonder, I would open my cupped hands to show you the breathless beauty I have captured somewhere out there in the world, my firefly of wonder, my freckle-faced smile, my heart.

My Quiet Place,
My Still, Oh Where?

Consistency is simply not my forte — not my strength.

    So much I wish.

    So much I want.

The hours of stillness before everyone is up, before all the needs
of everyone start piling up before me.

    So much I wish.

    So much I want.

But not enough apparently, if longing for and wishing, wanting
for

was deep enough, long enough, high enough, full and pouring
over,

I would find the time, make the time, create minutes out of

breaths between, store them in my pocket and pull them out,

stitch them together to embroider a moment

with pen and paper

to wrap my thoughts around words

to poise and perch and leap

at the page

my heart

    Splat

right there on the page

a big mess of bright colors

of wants and needs and loves and hopes
and my voice singing boldly
from amidst the jumbled,
busy, happy deluge of color
and water and fountains
of words dancing in the light
splashing and spraying and laughing.

And my children are loud and crazy
in the next room, ready to topple me
with play. It is the weekend, my time
to hold them, and wrestle and run after them
days on end for fun. I am filled up from a moment
of writing — my heart is in balance
and I am off to be a mommy!

Sink Down Deep

What does it mean to sink down deep
into who you are and speak your truth
and be yourself, and have your own
moment of HOWL, to sound your own
Barbaric Yawp over the rooftops of the world?

It may mean to say without thinking,
recite without reading, or read
without looking up once because
the words on the page and you are one,
the rhythm inherent in your tone and
your caress of this word and then the next;
the shape of your voice, the curve
of your neck, your hand outstretched
behind you in a bit of a tense,
in a bit of a grip, in that moment
as the words spill out —
Because this is where you live.

This is your moment and here we are
to hear you laugh or cry or speak in whispers.
We are here to listen and nod along
and take in all that you will pour out to us.
This is where you leave it all on the stage —

your anger, your frustration, the haunting play
of melody in your timbre, your rhythmic dance,
the way your voice almost cracks as you're
about to cry, and we all do an audible intake of breath
to be with you in that place of hurt or bliss,
pain and freedom and rage and "Here it is,
my raw, my beauty, my private, but
something I know we all share."

This is what it is to touch a cord;
to speak something universal and real
and wicked close to heart.

This is what it is to sink down deep
to find the place where words
reverberate against your ribcage
and holler out and grab others
to shake the bars and stomp the feet
in solidarity of YES!
This is what I speak tonight.
Do you hear me?

The Secret Life of Words

Ever since declaring herself a Poet
the words had ceased to spill
onto the page. They now hung
just above, in midair,
twirling in the dusty sunbeams,
bewildered by ineffectiveness,
stunned by their own silence.

Many took the opportunity,
not often afforded to words,
to languish and lollygag in their
suspended purgatory.

There were the clown-around words
who imagined themselves
chubby cupids and aimed spit wads
at one another for lack of arrows.

The melancholy words curled
up limply and allowed a slow,
steady supply of tears to fall
onto the page making patterns.

The more interpretive words

tried to analyze the splotches,
and ended up being convinced
every blot was suggestive and seductive
and pointed to something
pent-up in the weeper.

There were words who liked
to be in charge and tried to create
order by pushing and shoving
and aiming one word at another
effectively bouncing words around
in space like pool balls colliding
and spinning into pockets where
the edge of the page should be.

Meanwhile, the page itself grew
steadily more concerned, started crumpling
itself to add height and reach a few
of the low-hanging words and make
meaning of the mess.

Some of the young-hearted words
were relishing the naughtiness
of taunting the page with a near connect
and then a leap back higher
into the air — little air gymnasts,
all flip and swagger and free float.

She was surprised to see the secret
life of words when not being assigned
a place or function — how much fun
they had on their own.

This Page

(written about a long, long ago dark place)

This page, this page and I
we come together out of habit
and necessity. A pendulum rhythm
brings me back time and again.
A steady swing through ups and downs,
highs and lows, moments of
triumph, days of nothing much but
daydreaming on the way back to a
tragedy — a loss, a turn so sudden
the wind is knocked out of me
and I stagger to breathe. In those
dark depths, I have been
tempted... I have felt certain
I could bear no more. One sadness,
one period of darkness sat
so heavy on me, it felt impossible
to ever rise again. In devastation
so complete, I dragged myself
to the page to unpack this pain,
to try to hold on, to maybe find
a path to healing. I tried to
think of anything beautiful,

anything at all, and sobbed
when the idea of innocent
children popped into my head.
They are a result of connection — I
countered — and that
was the ache that gnawed at me,
the pain I felt would never go
away — a brutal act
that had broken me
beyond what I thought I could bear.
Now I sat torn and shattered
and holding onto a page
for dear life — thinking if I
picked up my pen from the page,
I would lose my mind — so
fragile and destroyed was I.
Flowers? No, they are a result
of pollination, which too is
connection of a kind. And my body
wracked with sobs as sanity
swirled around the edges of an
abyss I teetered on, my mind
could grasp at nothing beautiful
that would offer me sanctuary
and a place to recover. My
pen made dancing scribbles down
the page as I sobbed. I was unsure
if I would exist beyond this
moment if my pen left the page;
so sure was I that my mind
was ready to burst into fragments
of pain. I don't know how long I sat

sobbing, pen to paper, unravelling.
The lightning strike pattern
on the page brought me back
from the edge. The knowledge
that this page had saved me —
that staying true to the artist heart
that beat inside me and refusing to
break from my process of Good-Go to
the Page, Bad-Go to the Page, Destroyed
Beyond Recognition-to the page, damn it all.
The page and the pen and the lightning
and the dance of spirit and sadness
and madness and hope gave me solace,
reminded me of my purpose and my place.
Right here on this page — with pen moving
is where I belong. It is where beauty
can save me.

Craft

(for Mia Paschal — after she performed a teaser of her One-Woman-Show at a Fresno Rogue Festival event in 2008)

There you stood,
a tiny figure bathed in light
in the center of a dark stage,
perfectly still.

You stood silent
moments longer than you needed to,
just to get our attention.

It wasn't nerves, it was
perfection. It was a cat
about to pounce. It was
you with a pout on your lips,
and a gleam in your eye,
and then stronger
than anyone could have
imagined,
your voice split the stage
and hair stood up
on the backs of necks
all over the room.

You became motion
and light and swirls of wonder,
a dancer, a wood nymph,
the Angel of Death,
and Tinkerbell all
wrapped into one.
You were laughter
and pain together.
You were a dare
and truth in one breath.

You licked your wounds
in front of us all,
then pulled yourself up straight,
your tail curled 'round you
like an opera gown,
and batted your beautiful eyes.
A smirk, a glimmer,
a Broadway bow,
a regal exit stage left,
and we were left
scooping our chins off the ground.

Wonder at the
Whimsy of Others

(A meditation on some of the members of our Rogue Poetry
Slam — Southern Oregon Poetry Group)

I wonder what it would be like to be inside
Alexandra's mind — with lush flowers trailing
from ancient urns in a wild table display,
berries bursting with color tucked in among
sumptuous cheeses. Long chains of pearls,
and longer still legs and ankles, curled up
with a classic text, my girl sighs over
turns of phrases rich and drenched in
steamy subplot. Her pen in hand, she
moves us to the dark side, the breathless side,
the pain and the pleasure, the thorns and roses, or the
Slow, Sweet, Southern Magnolia Smiles.

I daydream about being inside
the poet heart of Shira, who tumbles
among the lines of her poems, tiptoeing,
dancing, sidling up to an idea and winking,
then waltzing away to turn around
and crash into it again — full frontal

and kiss on the lips and little moans,
grabbing it around the waist for emphasis.
Her words float and flirt and fly
straight at the sun.

I am in awe of Gene Burnett and his way
with rhyme and rhythm, his nuance, his
vast knowledge of every artistic superhero,
their backstory, their undiscovered genius:
  "Picasso Incognito."
And his truth and love and his smitten kitten
yowling for his lady when she's
away and studying.

I am blessed by Blaine, as he channels
the phrasing, the lilt and passion
of Walt Whitman; his eyes closed, his head
turned up, his hands swaying as he rocks
up onto the balls of his feet to get closer
to the muse of sun & sky & water drops
of petals trailing on long branches
into the stream to speak
ever so much more than words alone.

Or Stew, our physics professor, crossdresser,
boondocks dweller— spinning theorems and widgets
and things too glorious for me to comprehend
but he breaks it down, and runs out of breath
to tell us, to tell us with all his might,
that science is beautiful, and we
are beautiful, we are burning bright
particles of stars and wonders if we

would just let ourselves know it.
He held my hands until they stopped shaking
after I shared in this room
something so scary I couldn't breathe.

I sit on the edge of my seat to hear our young poets
who can whip out raps and dazzle and disorient us
and speak their truth and their pain in rat-a—tat strain,
who share their triggers, their exile,
their healing, their falling down again.

And our host, T Poe, who stands still before us
at the mic and wages battle with every perfect line
and every ship shape, dress right, open wound,
insert vice, struggle to breathe with bayonet overhead
and waters chest high and heart that has broken
and wanted to die but damn straight wouldn't keel over.

My gallery could go on and on with poet friends
and the gifts they bestow on us. These are the
deacons and elders of my Holy Poetry Church.

Once a Black Sheep

For those of us who have had
to create our own families
along the way
because we either didn't fit —
we weren't the missing puzzle piece —
in our original family, or
there was no puzzle to begin with —
just a blank page, blank stares
and rough handling.

Our crooked edges continually reinforced
our need to be reshaped, smoothed,
formed into what *would* work — the words
that would confirm our true belonging
stuck in our throats
and refused to form on our tongues.

For most of us, there were years
of attempting and constant rebuttals or
rejections, our trying was not good enough,
just *trying* in the maddening, disturbing,
eye-rolling way.

All through our first few decades

we struggled: we took wrong paths, hung with
the wrong crowds, wore the wrong clothes,
had the utterly wrong hair styles.
And we pushed the edges
because the edges seemed arbitrary
and ridiculous. The edges were random.
"You can go this far, and no farther,"
when out on the horizon was all the
adrenaline, all the hype,
the joy, the danger, and adventure.
All the things we craved were beyond
acceptable boundaries and we balked.
We raged against restrictions
and grew enormous wings
to fly over, beyond, out and above.
We soared. Sometimes we got help
from substances that are good at helping
angry, hopeless, forlorn people
soar away from bad places.

Sometimes the flying high was a good thing.
Sometimes we crashed. Sometimes we fell hard
and dug ourselves under rocks. We hid.
We drew damage to ourselves;
we hugged hard places close to us because
hard and bad were what we knew.

Until we stopped.

Because if we survived
all that garbage in our early years,
and we still had a desire

to fly and see beauty, we found a way.
We found our community,
our family of fabrication,
where other Black Sheep were in residence
and we fell in step with an out-of-step
syncopation that made sense
in its acceptance of nonsense.
And we stopped worrying what our family
of origin thought of us, because
they had placed their labels on us
and no matter what we achieved in life — they
would only ever see us as a bad example.
"Once a Black Sheep, always a Black Sheep."

We learned to see ourselves through the eyes
of Desire — all we ever wanted to be.
Every grand illusion, delusion or proclamation,
every vivid vision etched into our hearts.
We learned to see that the dream alone,
the ability to have that dream in that heart
in the first place,
was proof of all our possibilities.

Grace Falls

There is a loneliness inherent
in being a Poet.
Quiet time, away from others
is required.
We are the reflecting pool
of the world.
We speak the crumbling
mountains others see.
When pain is present
we slice to the center
to discover the filling
and taste the juices.
We are hollowed out,
scraped clean of every last
pumpkin seed and carved upon,
the faces to show with candles.
We are emptied out and wrung dry,
and left for dead.
These sacred, beating words
upon our temples.

We feel twice each moment,
full and reverberating
through our clerestory hearts.

Our words create pilgrimage sites,
Basilicas others travel to again
and again to drink in
the mysteries of the world.

There is hunger too, and nakedness,
there is raving mad and broken.
There is clawing, there is
scuttling across the sands
for hermit crab peace in burial.

And there is homecoming for even us.
Yes, Peace, Child, there is Here.
There is within this circle, an enclave,
and holy space. This unwinding
of tightened fists and hearts
closed for the depth of hurt,
the splendor sometimes
too much for us — the extremes
of cold and want and joy and plenty
wear us down and our words
catch in our throats — our prophet eyes
get grey from seeing too much
and we need our own
healing, our own place to recover.

Here, we break down, here others catch us.
We have been strong for too long,
speaking pains and breakthroughs
for others revivals, and we need
our own crying room and outstretched
hearts and soft shoulders to fall upon.

Eyes light with recognition, spirits soar
and swoop and dance
among the colonnades and rose windows,
our space to be heard more deeply
because other poets do the listening;
the fingers snapping, hand wave of Bravo,
Here where Grace Falls like
Gentle Rain on Tender Plants.